VAT &
Government
Departments

Martin Kaney BA LLB (Hons)

x-vat

Published August 2015 by

Spiramus Press Ltd
102 Blandford Street
London W1U 8AG
United Kingdom

www.spiramus.com

© Spiramus Press Ltd

Paperback   ISBN 9781907444098

Ebook   ISBN 9781904905431

This book is based on published HMRC and Treasury guidance and policy and on current case law and legislation in force as at 30 April 2015.

Printed and bound in Great Britain by Berforts Information Press, Stevenage, UK

About the author

Martin Kaney is the founder of the online VAT resource, X-VAT.

He has over 30 years' experience in the tax including eight years with HM Customs & Excise in VAT control and enforcement (with four years as a fraud and money laundering investigator in the Investigation Division) and various senior roles with Liaison, RSM Tenon and latterly, Deloitte.

He is a graduate of Edinburgh University, a member of the VAT Practitioners Group, a council member of the Gerson Lehrman Group, a provisional member of the Expert Witness Institute and an associate member of the Healthcare Financial Management Association, as well as holding an external law degree from Strathclyde University.

He is also the author of *VAT & the NHS* (Spiramus, second edition, 2015).

Acknowledgements

My thanks are due to my VAT colleague, Malcolm Comrie, for his help and technical comments in preparing *VAT & Government Departments* for publication.

Contents

CONTENTS

CONTENTS

Tables of authorities
Statutes

Regulations

Rules

Treatises

1   Value Added Tax

1.1   Introduction

Value Added Tax is a transaction tax on the supply of goods or services for the purpose of business charged by businesses to consumers as part of sales income. It is a self-assessed indirect tax on consumption, theoretically a tax borne by the final consumer (that is, a person who cannot claim it back). As a transaction tax it is not a tax on profits and the concept of profit has no meaning in VAT; liability is not calculated on net values (as opposed to determination of the amount due to be paid) but rather on the full value of supplies made or received (although, as always in VAT, there are exceptions to the general rule).

VAT was introduced in 1973 when the UK joined the then Common Market and it is the principal funding mechanism of the European Union (the term EC is still in use in relation to VAT), as well as being used as a form of taxation in up to 150 countries worldwide, including all of the OECD countries except the USA. VAT in the UK is ultimately governed by EU law (the *Principal VAT Directive 2006/112/EC*) though all Member States enact their own legislation interpreting the Directive (known as indirect effect). Where there is a conflict UK law is subordinate to EU law (although UK taxpayers are entitled to rely on domestic law until it is changed). In the UK the primary legislation is the Value Added Tax Act 1994 although there are various other Statutory Instruments and Regulations (notably the *VAT Regulations 1995 SI 1995/2518*), collectively known as secondary legislation. In addition, some HMRC publications have the force of law (tertiary legislation) and amendments are regularly made via the annual Finance Acts (changes to secondary or tertiary legislation can be made at any time).

1.1.1   The scope of VAT

The scope of VAT is defined in s.4 of the Act:
(1) VAT shall be charged on any supply of goods or services made in the United Kingdom, where it is a taxable supply made by a taxable person in the course or furtherance of any business carried on by him.
(2) A taxable supply is a supply of goods or services made in the United Kingdom other than an exempt supply.

Thus the scope of the tax is very wide and includes all activities in the course of business (or "economic activities" as defined in the Principal VAT Directive).

All supplies of goods or services made in the course or furtherance of business are taxable supplies unless they are specifically excluded such as the reduced-rate supplies listed in VAT Act 1994 Schedule 7A, the zero-rated supplies listed in VAT Act 1994 Schedule 8 and the exempt supplies listed in VAT Act 1994 Schedule 9. Exempt supplies are business activities within the scope of the tax but excluded from the charge to tax in s.4 by Schedule 9 and these include supplies of land or property (though this can also be taxable in certain circumstances), education, financial services, welfare and healthcare. Any person can make a taxable supply but only a taxable person (i.e. a legal person registrable under the Act – for example, any person or group of persons – a sole trader, partnership or corporate body) is required or able to charge VAT when making a taxable supply. All Government Departments (GDs) are registered for VAT as "bodies governed by public law" (*Principal VAT Directive*).

The scope of the tax is defined by HMRC as:
- a supply of goods or services;
- which takes place in the UK;
- and is made by a taxable person (someone who is, or is required to be registered); and
- is made in the course or furtherance of any business carried on or to be carried on by that person.

All four conditions must be met or the transaction or activity is outside the scope of UK VAT. For GDs the key condition is whether or not an activity is carried on in the course or furtherance of business or whether it is non-business (i.e. a statutory function or carried on for no consideration).

1.1.2 General principles

VAT as a tax may be summed up as a value added charge on:

WHO supplies **WHAT** to **WHOM, WHY, WHEN, WHERE** and for **HOW MUCH**…
- the **WHO** is the person who makes the supply – VAT is only chargeable by taxable persons – even then the status of the person making the supply can determine the VAT liability;
- the **WHAT** is what is supplied i.e. goods or services – anything which is not a supply of goods is a supply of services (unless there is a defined exclusion or for services no consideration i.e. nothing received in return);
- the **WHOM** is the person who receives the supply of goods or services – the status of the person who receives a supply can determine the VAT liability;
- the **WHY** is the purpose of the supply – is it business or non-business?

- the **WHEN** is when the supply becomes chargeable to tax – this is called the tax point and this determines the VAT period in which it should be accounted for – and whether the supply is out of time;
- the **WHERE** is where the supply is made (or deemed to be made) – the liability can be affected either by where the supplier is based or where the recipient is based (or whether the supply is one of goods or services);
- the **HOW MUCH** is the consideration for the supply – whatever is received in return i.e. anything received including barter, not just money (although it must be capable of expression as a monetary value).

All of the above are aspects of supply, the fundamental concept of the tax:
- **WHO?** – the person who makes the supply
- **WHAT?** – the type of supply
- **WHOM?** – the recipient of the supply
- **WHY?** – the purpose of the supply
- **WHEN?** – the time of supply
- **WHERE?** – the place of supply
- **HOW MUCH?** – the value of the supply

The VAT liability of any transaction can be analysed (and therefore understood) in the context of these defining questions. If supply is the fundamental concept of the tax the charge to tax (output tax) arises as a value added charge on a relevant transaction (i.e. within the scope of the tax and a taxable supply).

Tax which is charged out on business income is called output tax (there are currently three positive rates of tax: standard @ 20%; reduced @ 5%; and zero @ 0%). Tax which is incurred on business expenditure is called input tax. The net amounts of income or expenditure (i.e. the relevant sums exclusive of VAT) are called outputs (business income) and inputs (business expenditure) respectively and the net amount payable or repayable in the VAT Return is the amount of credit for input tax allowable (not all input tax is allowable) deducted from the total output tax payable.

Allowable input tax (*VAT Act 1994 s.26*) means VAT incurred which is attributable:
- to taxable supplies of goods and services made in the UK; or
- to supplies made outside the UK which would be taxable supplies if made in the UK (including within and outside the EU); or
- to exempt supplies within the de minimis limits.

Input tax attributable to exempt supplies outside the de minimis limits is not allowable (more than £7,500 p.a. and not more than 50% of the total input tax incurred).

VAT is unique in having the dual output and input perspective. All other taxes (including other indirect taxes) only have a single focus, but in VAT the output tax and input tax implications of any transaction must always be considered because the scope of the tax is so wide. This fundamental aspect of the tax is often overlooked, even by VAT professionals and HMRC. It is not unusual to find a transaction which has only been considered from either the output or the input perspective but not both simultaneously. Understanding the duality of the tax is the key to understanding the tax itself and making informed decisions.

1.1.3   Meaning of business

The meaning of business is not comprehensively defined in the VAT Act 1994 or the Principal VAT Directive despite its significance to the scope of the tax.

There is a partial definition in VAT Act 1994 s.94:

S.94 Meaning of "business" etc.

(1) In this Act "business" includes any trade, profession or vocation.

(2) Without prejudice to the generality of anything else in this Act, the following are deemed to be the carrying on of a business—
  a.   the provision by a club, association or organisation (for a subscription or other consideration) of the facilities or advantages available to its members; and
  b.   the admission, for a consideration, of persons to any premises.

(3) [repealed by FA 1999]

(4) Where a person, in the course or furtherance of a trade, profession or vocation, accepts any office, services supplied by him as the holder of that office are treated as supplied in the course or furtherance of the trade, profession or vocation.

(5) Anything done in connection with the termination or intended termination of a business is treated as being done in the course or furtherance of that business.

(6) The disposition of a business as a going concern, or of its assets or liabilities (whether or not in connection with its reorganisation or winding up), is a supply made in the course or furtherance of the business.

A series of tests (now collectively known as "the business test") has been developed:

- is the activity a "serious undertaking earnestly pursued" or a "serious occupation not necessarily confined to commercial or profit making undertakings"?
- is the activity an occupation or function actively pursued with reasonable or recognisable continuity?
- does the activity have a certain measure of substance as measured by the quarterly or annual value of taxable supplies?
- is the activity conducted in a regular manner and on sound and recognised business principles?
- is the activity predominantly concerned with the making of taxable supplies to consumers for a consideration?
- are the taxable supplies of a kind which are commonly made by those who seek to profit by them?
- are others are carrying on the same type of activity and clearly doing so on a commercial basis?

Profit of itself is not definitive in determining whether an activity is carried on in the course or furtherance of business. Although VAT Act 1994 s.41(2) was repealed in Finance Act 2012 supplies between GDs remain subject to the Treasury Directions on deemed business activities and therefore activities which may not have been carried on in the course or furtherance of business are treated as business activities in this context (see **Chapter 4 Business Activities**).

1.1.4   Meaning of supply

There is no specific definition of supply in the VAT Act 1994 or the Principal VAT Directive but it includes all forms of supply but not anything done otherwise than for a consideration (e.g. services provided for no consideration). A supply must be a supply of goods or of services to fall within the scope of the tax and the Treasury may, by order, deem any transaction to be a supply of goods or of services or vice versa. Alternatively a supply may be neither a supply of goods or services and thus outside the scope of the tax e.g. transfer of a going concern.

A supply with various components may be either a single (or composite) supply or a multiple (or mixed) supply. Regard has to be given to all of the circumstances; a supply must normally be regarded as distinct and independent; a supply should not be artificially split; and, where there are component elements consideration should be given as to whether each component supply could be regarded as a principal supply or whether merely ancillary (but a single price is not definitive).

1.1.5 Meaning of consideration

Consideration is not defined in the VAT Act 1994 or the Principal VAT Directive but is given the following meaning in the EC Second Directive (normally relied upon):

> "everything received in return for the supply of goods or the provision of services, including incidental expenses (packing, transport, insurance etc.) that is to say not only the cash amounts charged, but also, for example, the value of goods received in exchange or, in the case of goods or services supplied by order of a public authority, the amount of compensation received"

Thus, the definition is very wide and includes barter or an exchange of services etc. Consideration does not have to be a monetary payment but it must be capable of expression in a monetary value. Also, for a payment to be a consideration within the scope of the tax there must be a direct and immediate link to the supply.

1.1.6 A Government Department (GD) VAT overview

Public sector organisations (or "bodies governed by public law" in EU terminology) must be registered for VAT where they engage in "economic activities" (i.e. business activities for UK VAT purposes), especially where there is any competition with the private sector (*Article 13, Principal VAT Directive*).

For GDs VAT has two distinct aspects, the first being the special rules for GDs (and the NHS) under VAT Act 1994 s.41 (the Treasury (Contracting-Out) Directions) known as the contracted-out services or COS rules (in relation to non-business activities), the second being Value Added Tax itself, governed by the VAT legislation (in relation to business activities). Section 41 is a public policy compensation scheme which only applies in relation to non-business activities and VAT which is refunded under s.41 is not tax, but rather a refund of the amount of the tax charged. Specifically, it is not input tax which can only be incurred in relation to business activities (*VAT in the Public Sector and Exemptions in the Public Interest* TAXUD/2009/DE/316).

The s.41 special legal regime applies to GDs in England, Scotland and Wales but Northern Ireland has its own special legal regime under VAT Act 1994 s.99. The essential difference is that while s.41 refunds only apply to VAT on a list of eligible services published by the Treasury s.99 refunds apply to VAT on both goods and services. The s.41 special legal regime also applies to the NHS in England, Scotland and Wales but the s.99 special legal regime applies to the NHS in Northern Ireland. Relief for Non-Departmental Public Bodies (NDPBs) operating in a shared service context was announced in the Budget 2015 but is currently deferred (the proposed s.33E).

In addition to s.41 and s.99 there is another special legal regime under VAT Act 1994 s.33 which applies to local, fire and police authorities as well as other specified public sector bodies. Again, the essential difference is that s.33 refunds apply to VAT on both goods and services and there are also special partial exemption rules. It is important not to confuse these regimes (because the rules are different and give rise to different outcomes) but at the same time important to understand the differences because of their interaction in a public sector context (for example, a partnership project between a GD and a local authority will give rise to a different VAT position for each partner with a potential impact on funding requirements). Relief under s.33 was extended to search and rescue charities, palliative care charities and medical courier charities from 1 April 2015.

There is no overlap between the VAT regime and the s.41 special legal regime; these are mutually exclusive. To understand VAT in a GD context it is essential to understand this second fundamental duality in the tax in relation to the public sector. Again, this is often overlooked and because in certain situations VAT can apparently be recovered in both contexts COS eligibility to recover and input tax entitlement on VAT incurred can be confused. The VAT legislation and input tax entitlement always take precedence over the Treasury (Contracting-Out) Directions and eligibility to make a claim (because domestic UK legislation is subordinate to EU law). The distinction is important because if the VAT incurred is not correctly characterised it may lead to compliance errors and affect the amount of VAT a GD is able to claim back overall.

VAT & Government Departments is intended to be both a reference manual and a practical guide to managing VAT for GDs (there is a list of References at **Appendix 10**: References). Many of the areas covered in the text are complex in themselves and *VAT & Government Departments* does not attempt to examine all possibilities in all circumstances or to reproduce the full technical guidance or statute. Rather the objective is to identify all of the issues in the tax relevant to GDs and in a logical analysis explain these from a compliance perspective and in relation to the organisational activities of GDs (providing further references where appropriate if more detailed information is required). GDs are different from each other in the activities they undertake (since by definition each GD exists to carry out specific functions) but there are significant areas of overlap such as land and property (see **Chapter 5 Land and Property**) or international transactions (see **Chapter 6 International VAT**). This book cannot deal with the specifics of each type of activity but it does cover the main areas of activity where issues are likely to arise. If in doubt, it should always be remembered that any activity on the Treasury List (see **Chapter 4 Business Activities**) is likely to be business (or deemed to be business) and any business activity in the UK is standard-rated unless specifically excluded in the Schedules to the VAT Act 1994.

To read VAT Notices or other VAT Guidance referenced in the text:
https://www.gov.uk/business-tax/vat

To read the full text of UK Statutes referenced in the text:
http://www.legislation.gov.uk

GD VAT has recently been the subject of an HMRC consultation and review with new guidance published in 2015 (consolidated with revised NHS guidance) and as always in VAT there are various areas of uncertainty and unresolved issues and this is in the nature of the tax which is constantly evolving through case law and new legislation. *VAT & Government Departments* is based on published HMRC and Treasury guidance and policy and on current case law and legislation in force as at 30 April 2015.

1.2   VAT & Government Departments

For GDs VAT is administered by the HMRC Government Departments Team (within the Public Bodies Group) and every GD should have a Customer Relations Manager (CRM) or Customer Co-ordinator in the Government Departments Team. The Treasury determines policy in relation to COS and this is administered and implemented by HMRC on its behalf. VAT policy is determined by HMRC in accordance with the VAT legislation. VAT policy applies to GDs subject to the VAT legislation in relation to activities within the scope of tax i.e. in relation to output tax and input tax and business activities but not in relation to COS or non-business activities. However, GDs are also subject to certain unique policy restrictions, for example, they are only permitted to opt to tax property with the permission of Treasury and as a matter of policy rather than law they are not allowed to carry out partial exemption calculations (but see **1.2.2 Trading funds** below).

As bodies governed by public law all GDs are taxable persons and all are thus registered for VAT (the normal registration limits do not apply). All GDs are separate taxable persons and supplies between them are subject to VAT in the normal way. When a GD registers for VAT it is given a 3 digit number but will also be automatically assigned a 9 digit number (which starts with 888). The 9 digit number is unique to the GD to which it is issued. This number must be shown on all tax invoices and correspondence relating to taxable supplies made. Executive Agencies and Trading Funds are normally part of their parent GD for VAT purposes. GDs must use their 9 digit number on tax invoices issued in relation to sales. When trading with other Member States or importing or exporting goods they will be given a separate VAT registration number which should be used in these circumstances. This number must be prefixed with "GB". Confirmation of GD VAT registration numbers may be obtained from the Government Departments Team. The Northern Ireland Executive is registered under a single VAT registration number assigned to the Department of Finance and Personnel which manages the finances of all departments.

Like all taxable persons GDs are required to maintain a VAT Account and the figures from the VAT Account are transferred to the online VAT Return. The VAT Account is a summary of all transactions in the source ledgers and accounts e.g. the value of taxable and exempt supplies and corresponding output tax, the value of purchases attributable to business activities both taxable and exempt and input tax and COS claimed etc. In addition, adjustments e.g. journals or other adjustments such as the correction of errors are shown in the VAT Account. Whilst not strictly necessary it is also good practice to include non-business income and non-business expenditure.

All GDs submit online VAT Returns based on calendar months (monthly or quarterly). GD VAT Returns are the same as for any other taxable person but GDs are also required to complete a VAT 21 form (to be completed online with the VAT Return) which identifies both the value of input tax claimed and the value of the refund claimed under each COS Heading. Output tax should be charged at the appropriate rate (standard, reduced or zero) where applicable and declared on the relevant VAT Return. Input tax should be deducted where applicable and allowable (e.g. VAT incurred in relation to a business activity). COS entitlement should be quantified according to each individual Heading and claimed on the online VAT 21 (automatically included in the online VAT Return).

All GDs and Executive Agencies or Trading Funds separately registered for VAT are required to appoint a VAT Liaison Officer and it is the responsibility of the VLO to act as the internal point of contact and advice on VAT.

The role of the VLO is an onerous one because HMRC expects the VLO to ensure that:
(a) the GD or separately registered Executive Agency or Trading Fund reclaims or pays the correct amount of VAT;

(b) the list of business activities in the annual Taxing Direction is kept up to date and that HMRC are informed as soon as a change occurs;

(c) HMRC is made aware at an early stage of any initiatives that a GD or separately registered Executive Agency or Trading Fund is planning or about to announce (so as to be able to advise on the VAT implications for funding purposes).

1.2.1 Executive agencies

As a matter of law Executive Agencies are part of government. Executive Agencies which operate under the GD VAT registration number of the parent GD should use that VAT registration number in relation to any supplies made and are included in the reference to the parent GD in the list of eligible departments (see **Appendix 6**) in the Treasury (Taxing) Directions and the Treasury (Contracting-Out) Directions (and therefore do not submit separate VAT returns to HMRC although there may be an internal VAT return to the parent GD). Supplies between an Executive Agency and its parent GD are disregarded but the normal rules apply when supplies are made to an external recipient.

HMRC will consider requests for separate VAT registration if the request is endorsed and supported by the parent GD. If separate GD VAT registration is granted to an Executive Agency it will be treated as a separate GD for VAT purposes. A separately registered Executive Agency must appoint a VLO, have its own reference in the Treasury (Taxing) Directions and it must request that HMRC add it to the list of eligible departments (see **Appendix 6**) for the Treasury (Contracting-Out) Directions (for the refund of VAT on services related to its non-business activities). Supplies between a separately registered Executive Agency and the parent GD are generally business activities and VAT is chargeable subject to the normal rules.

1.2.2 Trading funds

As a matter of law Trading Funds are part of government. Trading Funds which operate under the GD VAT registration number of the parent GD should use that VAT registration number in relation to any supplies made and are included in the reference to the parent GD in the list of eligible departments (see **Appendix 6**) in the Treasury (Taxing) Directions and the Treasury (Contracting-Out) Directions (and therefore do not submit separate VAT returns to HMRC although there may be an internal VAT return to the parent GD). Supplies between a Trading Fund and its parent GD are disregarded but the normal rules apply when supplies are made to an external recipient.

HMRC will consider requests for separate VAT registration if the request is endorsed and supported by the parent GD. If separate GD VAT registration is granted to a Trading Fund it will be treated as a separate GD for VAT purposes. A separately registered Trading Fund must appoint a VLO, have its own reference in the Treasury (Taxing) Directions. Supplies between a separately registered Trading Fund and the parent GD are generally business activities and VAT is chargeable subject to the normal rules. A Trading Fund is normally only involved in business activities and it is likely that a Trading Fund will not be in a position to recover any VAT under the Treasury (Contracting-Out) Directions. Where a Trading Fund is engaged in making exempt supplies as well as taxable supplies then it may, subject to approval by the Treasury and in conjunction with the Government Departments Team, adopt a partial exemption method which will enable it to apportion its input tax.

1.2.3 Non-departmental public bodies
The definition of an NDPB is:

> "A body which has a role in the processes of national government, but is not a government department, or part of one, and which accordingly operates to a greater or lesser extent at arm's length from ministers."

In England the Cabinet Office decides which organisations are classified as NDPBs, in Scotland, the Scottish Government; in Wales, the Welsh Government; and, in Northern Ireland, the Northern Ireland Executive. NDPBs are not eligible for refunds under VAT Act 1994 s.41 and are subject to the normal VAT rules (albeit their activities are mostly non-business). An NDPB which is registered for VAT can recover the VAT incurred on the purchase, importation or acquisition of taxable goods and services attributable to its taxable activities (subject to the normal rules).

The UK Government classifies NDPBs into four different categories (the Scottish Government has a fifth category for NHS bodies):
(1) Advisory NDPBs – consisting of boards which advise ministers on particular policy areas (normally with admin and clerical support from the parent GD).
(2) Executive NDPBs – these bodies usually deliver a particular public service and are overseen by a board rather than ministers (normally with their own staff and budgets).
(3) Tribunal NDPBs – these bodies have jurisdiction in an area of the law (co-ordinated by the Tribunals Service, an Executive Agency of the Ministry of Justice, and supervised by the Administrative Justice and Tribunals Council, itself a NDPB sponsored by the Ministry of Justice).

(4) Independent Monitoring Boards – formerly known as "boards of visitors" these bodies are responsible for the state of prisons, their administration and the treatment of prisoners (normally funded by the Home Office).

The majority of NPDBs are wholly non-business and cannot register for VAT because they make no taxable supplies. However, it was announced in the Budget 2015 that certain NDPBs will in future be able to submit claims under VAT Act 1994 s.33E (similar to s.41) in relation to shared services, although this is currently deferred (see **Chapter 3 Contracted-Out Services**).

1.2.4   Northern Ireland

Northern Ireland Government Departments (GDNIs) are subject to the normal rules in relation to business activities (see **Chapter 4 Business Activities**) but VAT Act 1994 s.41 does not apply in Northern Ireland. Because GDNIs have a wider remit than GDs in England, Scotland or Wales (e.g. responsibility for education and healthcare) VAT Act 1994 s.99 is a special scheme for Northern Ireland (however, in the same way as NDPBs in England, Scotland and Wales are not eligible for refunds under VAT Act 1994 s.41, NDPBs in Northern Ireland are not eligible for refunds under s.99). VAT incurred on goods and services relating to non-business activities may be recovered under s.99.

Each GDNI is expected to have a method of business/non-business apportionment which gives a fair and reasonable result and which is agreed with the Department of Finance & Personnel in Northern Ireland. The non-business % is then applied to VAT incurred on purchases of goods or services in the UK and goods purchased from other Member States (or outside the EU). VAT incurred on services purchased from other Member States for non-business purposes cannot be recovered under s.99 because the refund scheme only applies to UK VAT.

1.2.5   Tax advisers

As a matter of Treasury policy public sector organisations are not permitted to "engage in, or connive at, tax evasion, tax avoidance or tax planning" on the basis that if a public sector organisation were to obtain financial advantage by moderating the tax paid by a contractor, supplier or other party it would normally have a negative effect on the public sector as a whole.

Thus any participation in artificial tax avoidance schemes should normally be rejected although certain tax planning schemes may be allowed with Treasury consent. It is recommended practice to consult HMRC about unusual transactions or non-standard approaches to tax before going ahead. Treasury allows the use of tax advisers to help meet the normal and legitimate requirements of carrying on public business such as the administration of VAT, PAYE and NICs, where expert assistance can be beneficial or enhance efficiency.

(see *Managing Public Money* (HM Treasury))

1.2.6   EU Principal VAT Directive

Article 13 of the EU Principal VAT Directive (previously Article 4(5) of the EC *Sixth VAT Directive - 77/388/EEC*) applies to bodies governed by public law as follows:

13(1) States, regional and local government authorities and other bodies governed by public law shall not be regarded as taxable persons in respect of the activities or transactions in which they engage as public authorities, even where they collect dues, fees, contributions or payments in connection with those activities or transactions.

However, where they engage in such activities or transactions, they shall be regarded as taxable persons in respect of those activities or transactions where there treatment as non-taxable persons would lead to significant distortion of competition.

In any event, bodies governed by public law shall be regarded as taxable persons in respect of the activities listed in Annex 1 provided that these activities are not carried out on such a small scale as to be negligible.

(2) Member states may regard activities , exempt under Articles 132, 135, 136, 371, 374, to 377 and Article 378(2), Article379(2), or Articles 380 to 390 engaged in by bodies governed by public law as activities in which those bodies engage as public authorities.

The consequence of Article 13(1) is that government and public bodies are not treated as taxable persons when they engage in certain activities or transactions and these activities or transactions are outside the scope of VAT, unless this would significantly distort competition. By 'taxable person' the EU legislation means a person who, independently, carries out an economic activity whatever the purpose or result of that activity.

Annex 1 to the *Principal VAT Directive* (PVD) lists the activities that will always be taxable when carried out by bodies governed by public law unless carried out on a negligible scale:

(1)   telecommunications;
(2)   supply of water, gas, electricity and thermal energy;
(3)   transport of goods;
(4)   port and airport services;
(5)   passenger transport
(6)   supply of new goods manufactured for sale;

(7) transactions in respect of agricultural products, carried out by agricultural intervention agencies pursuant to Regulations on the common organisation of the market in those products;

(8) organisation of trade fairs and exhibitions;

(9) warehousing;

(10) activities of commercial publicity bodies;

(11) activities of travel agencies;

(12) running of staff shops, cooperatives and industrial canteens and similar institutions;

(13) activities carried out by radio and television bodies in so far as these are not exempt pursuant to Article 132(1)(q).

1.2.7   Non-business activities

HMRC take the view that activities funded by taxation or wholly by central or local government for the wider public good will always be outside the scope of VAT because what is received by the public body is not consideration for a supply in the course or furtherance of business.

The basic principles for public sector non-business activities are that:
- bodies should form a part of the public administration;
- bodies should engage as public authorities for the activity in question, which means that the activity is governed by legislation which does not apply to non-public bodies;
- the activity is not listed in Annex I of the Principal VAT Directive; and
- the result should not significantly distort competition with non-public bodies.

Funding for the activities carried out by a public body under statutory powers may also come from a mixture of grants and statutory contributions by private individuals or businesses, where:
- money is given freely to an activity and the donor receives nothing tangible in return, the activity is treated as non-business for VAT purposes;
- a donation is given on the understanding that it is spent on a particular activity, it is non-business as long as the donor is receiving no direct benefit;
- an activity is funded wholly by statutory charge, or for which someone is legally required to contribute, it is non-business;
- there is a supply that is paid for and it is not voluntary or statutory, and where the person giving the money receives something tangible in return, it is treated as being made in the course or furtherance of business.

(see *HMRC VAT Manual VATGPB3000*)

2 Accounting for VAT

2.1 VAT Compliance

The primary objective of VAT accounting for GDs is compliance on the "right tax at the right time" principle. There is never an apportionment of output tax; it is always payable in full. However, there may be an apportionment of the VAT incurred by a GD between its business activities and non-business activities, firstly as input tax and then as COS. For policy reasons partial exemption does not apply to GDs i.e. where the VAT incurred is partly attributable to exempt supplies (although it is allowed for Trading Funds subject to the permission of Treasury and by agreement with the Government Departments Team). If VAT is incurred on purchases that are used for both taxable and exempt supplies none of it should be recovered as input tax (HMRC *Guidance Notes for Government Departments* 6th Edn Part 1.15). Essentially, output tax is straightforward according to the VAT liability of the supplies made but calculating how much of the VAT incurred can be reclaimed either as COS or input tax is a more complex process.

2.2 The VAT Account

Regulation 32 (*VAT Regulations 1995 SI 1995/2518*) provides that every taxable person must keep a VAT Account:

- the VAT Account is to be divided into separate parts for each prescribed accounting period (i.e. VAT Return period);
- the VAT Account is to be divided into two parts, the VAT payable portion and the VAT allowable portion;
- the VAT payable portion includes a total of all output tax due, including tax on acquisitions from other Member States, and all corrections or adjustments allowed or required in the VAT Regulations; and
- the VAT allowable portion includes a total of all input tax allowable under VAT Act 1994 s.26, including tax allowable on acquisitions from other Member States, and all corrections or adjustments allowed or required in the VAT Regulations.

Keeping a VAT Account is a statutory requirement but it is also the key to a fully compliant VAT accounting system. A comprehensive and compliant VAT Account is an effective mechanism to ensure that an accurate declaration of VAT is made. This not only reduces the risk of an error giving rise to potential penalties but should also downgrade an organisation's risk status according to HMRC criteria (potentially reducing the frequency or intensity of HMRC visits, for example).

The inclusion of s.41 refunds in the VAT Account is not mandatory because COS is outside the scope of VAT but it is good practice to include all income and all expenditure. In addition to output tax and input tax calculated under Regulation 32 this also allows for the completion of the VAT 21, current business/non-business apportionment, the inclusion of any other relevant adjustments (such as an approved error correction notification) and the final calculation of VAT due for the period plus any COS refund to be claimed.

2.3   Compliance Checklist

The basic compliance checks for the preparation of a VAT Return are set out below:

2.3.1   Preliminaries

Income – ensure that all income (including cash income) is recorded in the VAT Account whatever the source or liability – include all central funding and grants as well as income from business activities or charges to the public.

Expenditure – ensure that all expenditure is recorded in the VAT Account whatever the activity or purpose – include all expenditure and purchases.

Liability – having checked that all income and all expenditure has been included in the VAT Account the VAT liability of each income stream or line of expenditure should be reviewed to ensure that it is correctly characterised i.e. is the income consideration for a taxable or exempt supply, and if taxable, at which rate? – is it non-business or otherwise outside the scope of VAT? – is the expenditure attributable to a business activity, and if so, taxable or exempt? – is it attributable to non-business activities? – or is the income or expenditure non-attributable or partially attributable?

2.3.2   Outputs

Output tax – ensure that all output tax charged or chargeable on standard-rated taxable business activities is identified and included.

Reduced-rate – ensure that all reduced-rate income from taxable business activities is identified and that output tax is charged at the correct rate.

Zero-rated – ensure that all zero-rated income from taxable business activities is identified and that output tax is not charged.

Exempt – ensure that all income from exempt business activities is identified and included and that output tax is not charged.

Bad Debt Relief – ensure that any claims for bad debt relief are included.

Credit Notes – ensure that a credit note is created for any credit adjustment arising where a debtor has been overcharged (if applicable).

EU Removals (Goods) – any removals of goods to other Member States should be checked for the correct treatment (zero-rated when supplied to VAT registered businesses in another Member State) (see **Chapter 6 International VAT**).

Exports (Goods) – any transactions outside the EU should be checked – exports of goods outside the EU are zero-rated provided that appropriate evidence of export is obtained and there would be a corresponding Input tax entitlement under VATA 1994 s.26 (see **Chapter 6 International VAT**).

EU Reverse Charge (Services) – supplies of international services made (within the EU) – special care should be exercised over the supply of services made within the EU – there are complex rules on place of supply which determine in which Member State the VAT liability arises – where the place of supply is deemed to be another Member State the supply is outside the scope of UK VAT (Boxes 6 & 8 of the VAT Return) and the recipient would be required to account for the tax as a reverse charge (see **Chapter 6 International VAT**).

Non-EU Reverse Charge (Services) – supplies of international services made (outside the EU) – special care should be exercised over the supply of services outside the EU – these will normally be outside the scope of VAT (rather than zero-rated) but there will nevertheless be a corresponding entitlement to input tax under VAT Act 1994 s.26 provided the supply is attributable to a taxable business activity (see **Chapter 6 International VAT**).

2.3.3   Inputs

Input tax – ensure that all allowable input tax attributable to business activities is identified and claimed where attributable to taxable supplies.

Zero-rated Purchases – ensure that zero-rating has been correctly applied by the supplier for any other purchases where appropriate.

Reduced-rate Purchases – ensure that the reduced-rate has been correctly applied by the supplier for any other purchases where appropriate.

Debit Notes – ensure that a debit note is created for any debit adjustment arising from a creditor overcharge (if applicable).

EU Acquisitions (Goods) – any acquisition of goods from within the EU should be checked for the correct treatment (Box 2 of the VAT Return) – if the acquisition relates to a taxable supply or is recoverable as COS then

VAT should be reclaimed either as input tax or COS in Box 4 of the VAT Return (net value in Boxes 7 and 9) (see **Chapter 6 International VAT**).

Imports (Goods) – any transactions from outside the EU should be checked – there are various provisions related to the relief of VAT on the importation of goods but normally VAT would be payable on importation – any input tax entitlement would be based on the relevant import documentation (see **Chapter 6 International VAT**).

EU Reverse Charge (Services) – supplies of international services received (within the EU) – special care should be exercised over the supply of services received within the EU – there are general and special rules on the place of supply which determine in which Member State the VAT liability arises – where the place of supply is deemed to be the UK the VAT liability (output tax and input tax if appropriate) would have to be declared in the VAT Return (Boxes 1, 4, 6 & 7) (see **Chapter 6 International VAT**).

Non-EU Reverse Charge (Services) – supplies of international services received (from outside the EU) – special care should be exercised over the supply of services from outside the EU – with few exceptions the place of supply will be the UK under the EU VAT Package rules effective from 1 January 2010 and the VAT liability (output tax and input tax if appropriate) would have to be declared in the VAT Return (Boxes 1, 4, 6 & 7) (see **Chapter 6 International VAT**).

2.3.4 Contracted-out services
Contracted-Out Services – ensure that all COS entitlement for the period is identified and claimed.

EU & Non-EU Reverse Charge (COS) – include any COS entitlement arising from the output tax declared on eligible services received from either another Member State within the EU or outside (see Chapter 6 International VAT).

COS Underclaims – ensure that any COS underclaims for earlier periods are included (provided in time i.e. by 31 July following the end of the financial year).

COS Overclaims – ensure that any COS overclaims for earlier periods are included (HMRC do not apply the Treasury time limits to COS overclaims and will accept these out of time).

2.3.5 Finalisation
Journals – ensure that all journals have been taken into account.

Adjustments – a final check on adjustments – depending on which financial year it relates to a miscellaneous adjustment may have an effect on the annual adjustment for the current financial year or it may fall outside – if so, it may necessitate a further adjustment to an earlier financial year if the value is material.

VAT Account – a final check that all income, expenditure, supplies and activities, journals and adjustments have been taken into account.

Error Correction Notifications – check that any approved ECNs are not included – these are dealt with separately outside the VAT Returns because they are corrections to an earlier period.

Business/Non-Business Apportionment – check the business/non-business apportionment calculation where appropriate.

Partial Exemption – check the partial exemption calculation where appropriate (Trading Funds only).

VAT 21 – complete and submit the VAT 21 online.

VAT Return – complete and submit the VAT return online.

2.3.6   The VAT return

The VAT Return is the legal declaration of tax payable and tax allowable in any period. The content of a VAT Return is defined in Regulation 39 (*VAT Regulations 1995 SI 1995/2518*) and the definition does not include refunds under VAT Act 1994 s.41 (because these are not tax).

The VAT payable and VAT allowable portions of the VAT Account (Regulation 32 above) are carried through to the VAT Return:

In the box opposite the legend "VAT due in this period on sales and other outputs" shall be entered the aggregate of all the entries in the VAT payable portion of that part of the VAT account which relates to the prescribed accounting period for which the return is made, except that the total of the output tax due in that period on acquisitions from other Member States shall be entered instead in the box opposite the legend "VAT due in this period on acquisitions from other EC Member States".

In the box opposite the legend "VAT reclaimed in this period on purchases and other inputs" (including acquisitions from other Member States) shall be entered the aggregate of all the entries in the VAT allowable portion of that part of the VAT account which relates to the prescribed accounting period for which the return is made.

The VAT Return is the legal declaration of output tax and input tax due under the statutory VAT Regulations and the VAT Act 1994. Because s.41

refunds are outside the scope of VAT and do not form part of a Value Added Tax Return the inclusion of COS claims in the VAT Return is an administrative practice only (for the processing of repayments by HMRC).

The VAT 21 (headed "Certificate of VAT Reclaimed Under Section 41(3) of the VAT Act 1994") is a form devised by HMRC to itemise COS refunds claimed in any prescribed period (technically, it is not part of a VAT Return but is submitted at the same time). From 1 April 2010 VAT 21s and VAT Returns are submitted online and HMRC have produced a guide to assist (*A step by step guide to VAT online filing for Government Departments and NHS Trusts* (HMRC 2010)). The total sum for each COS Heading is calculated and submitted online in an analytical table. The VAT 21 also includes the total amount of "Input tax on Business activities" and the total amount claimed as COS is added to the input tax claim and automatically entered in Box 4 as part of the online submission process. Box 4 is calculated automatically from the VAT 21 entries. Boxes 3 and 5 are also automatically calculated when the remainder of the online VAT 100 has been completed.

The submission is finalised by electronic declarations that the information is "true and complete" with the obligatory warning that a "false declaration can result in prosecution". A VAT Return is a legal declaration and a significant responsibility for the authorised person who electronically "signs" or authorises it and it should be regarded as such.

Summary of VAT Return Boxes 1-9:

Box 1 – Output Tax

Box 2 – EU Acquisition Tax (tax chargeable on purchases of goods from other EU Member States)

Box 3 – Box 1 plus Box 2

Box 4 – Input Tax and COS

Box 5 – Box 3 minus Box 4

Box 6 – Outputs (net value of sales)

Box 7 – Inputs (net value of purchases)

Box 8 – EU Removals (net value of supplies of goods to other EU Member States)

Box 9 – EU Acquisitions (net value of purchases of goods from other EU Member States)

2.3.7 Error correction notifications

ECNs are required where there is an error in a previous VAT Return outside the limits below.

Method 1 – if the net value of errors is less than £10,000 or is between £10,000 and £50,000 but does not exceed 1% of outputs (the value of taxable and exempt supplies net of tax – Box 6 of the VAT Return for the period in which the errors were discovered) then the errors may be corrected directly on the VAT return without the requirement to submit an ECN (correction of an error using this Method does not constitute a disclosure for the purposes of VAT Penalties, this must be made separately, if appropriate).

Method 2 – if the net value of errors is between £10,000 and £50,000 and exceeds 1% of outputs (the value of taxable and exempt supplies net of tax – Box 6 of the VAT Return for the period in which the errors were discovered) or the net value of the errors is greater than £50,000 or the errors were made deliberately then an ECN is required. This can be made in writing or by submission of form VAT 652 to the Public Bodies Group.

2.3.8 Tax invoices

A Tax Invoice is the legal document which taxable persons must retain (for six years) as evidence of input tax entitlement (HMRC also require tax invoices to be retained for COS claims – although electronic storage is an option). A taxable person must supply another taxable person with a tax invoice where there has been a taxable supply. The requirement does not arise in relation to exempt supplies or non-business activities. If a GD makes a taxable supply to another taxable person then a tax invoice must be issued. There is no corresponding requirement where supplies are made to unregistered persons or private individuals e.g. cash income (but a taxable person is entitled to receive a tax invoice for a cash purchase from a GD if appropriate and this should be provided upon request).

A valid tax invoice requires:
- a sequential unique reference number
- time of supply i.e. tax point
- date of issue
- name, address and VAT registration number of supplier
- name and address of recipient
- description of goods or services supplied
- quantity of goods or extent of services, rate of VAT and amount payable excluding VAT
- unit price (if applicable)
- gross amount excluding VAT
- rate of any discount offered

- total amount of VAT chargeable

In certain circumstances self-billed invoices may be issued (where the recipient prepares the tax invoice on behalf of the supplier). Prior approval from HMRC is not required but certain conditions must be complied with (see *VAT Notice 700/62 Self-Billing*). Also where the consideration does not exceed £250 and the supply is within the UK a "less detailed" or simplified tax invoice can be issued (e.g. petrol receipts etc). All that is required for a simplified tax invoice is the name, address and VAT registration number of supplier, the time of supply, description of the goods or services, the total amount payable including VAT, the gross amount payable including VAT and the VAT rate applicable (see *VAT Notice 700 The VAT Guide*).

2.3.9 Error penalties

GDs became liable to the VAT penalty regime in 2011. If a GD takes reasonable care to complete the VAT Return but makes an error despite this it will not be liable to a penalty. The definition of 'reasonable care' varies according to circumstances but when taking reasonable care HMRC expect businesses to:

- make and keep sufficient records to provide a complete and accurate VAT Return;
- update records regularly;
- take tax seriously and take care to get it right.

A GD may be liable to a penalty if:

- the VAT Return is inaccurate and correcting this means tax is unpaid, understated, overclaimed or under-assessed; or
- HMRC are not informed within 30 days that a tax assessment is too low.

When assessing a penalty HMRC will explain:

- which error or errors made the GD liable to a penalty;
- the period the penalty applies to;
- the tax amount liable to a penalty;
- the amount of any reduction allowed;
- the amount of any penalty previously assessed for the period;
- the total amount of the penalty for the period;
- how and where to pay the penalty.

The penalty rate for an inaccurate VAT Return depends on why the error was made. The more serious the reason, the greater the penalty can be. The penalty is calculated as a percentage of the potential lost revenue i.e. the tax unpaid, understated, overclaimed or under-assessed, as a result of taxpayer errors.

HMRC have produced the table below in relation to penalties for errors in a VAT Return:

Reason for the error	Disclosure of the error to HMRC NB A disclosure is unprompted if at the time you tell HMRC about it you have no reason to believe HMRC have discovered it, or are about to discover it.	Minimum penalty (as a percentage of the tax)	Maximum penalty (as a percentage of the tax)
Careless (you fail to take reasonable care)	Unprompted	0%	30%
	Prompted	15%	30%
Deliberate (you give HMRC a document which you know contains an inaccuracy)	Unprompted	20%	70%
	Prompted	35%	70%
Deliberate and concealed (you give HMRC a document which you know contains an inaccuracy and you have tried to hide that inaccuracy)	Unprompted	30%	100%
	Prompted	50%	100%

If a penalty is a result of a "careless" error, HMRC can sometimes suspend it for up to two years. If HMRC can suspend a penalty, they will impose certain conditions that will help to avoid making the same error again. If it is not possible to set and agree these conditions a penalty cannot be suspended. If all of the conditions are met at the end of the suspension period HMRC will cancel the penalty provided the business does not become liable to another penalty during this period. HMRC cannot suspend a penalty that comes from 'deliberate' or 'deliberate and concealed' errors.

2.4   The VAT Management Plan

Creating a VAT Management Plan is good practice and enables the efficient management of VAT in relation to core activities and prudent VAT planning (it normally also results in improved levels of VAT recovery). It enables a GD to manage its relationship with HMRC and reduce risk. The plan should set out clear objectives in relation to the scheduling of core work and reviews, compliance checking procedures and planning opportunities.

A VAT Management Plan should include the following (on a financial year basis):

Update Meetings – the VAT Liaison Officer (VLO) should meet regularly with budget holders or finance managers to discuss developments and to update the VAT Management Plan for the coming financial year.

Compliance Systems – source data capture should be reviewed and checked to ensure that all data feeds through and that all formulas or calculations are correct and consistent.

VAT Account Review – the VAT Account should be checked to ensure that all formulas or calculations are correct and consistent.

VAT 21s Review – the VAT 21s should be checked to ensure that all formulas or calculations are correct and consistent.

VAT Returns Review – the VAT Returns should be checked to ensure that all formulas or calculations are correct and consistent.

COS Reviews – monthly, quarterly or annual schedule for reviewing COS claims – these should be planned in advance for the coming financial year.

July Deadline – backup reviews should be planned to ensure that all COS underclaims and overclaims have been finalised for 31 July each year.

Sales/Debtors Review – a review of outputs liabilities should be completed with particular emphasis on any new income streams – end of financial year.

Procurement Review – all capital expenditure on equipment, managed services contracts etc should be reviewed including any planned or future expenditure – with particular emphasis on any new procurements arising within the financial year.

Capital Planning Review – review the organisation's capital plans as far ahead as these are available e.g. three to five years if possible – this will enable informed consideration of the VAT implications on potentially significant expenditure to be undertaken at the earliest possible stage – in turn timeous VAT advice informs the decision making process.

Business Activities – review of business/non-business apportionment where appropriate – end of financial year.

Partial Exemption – review of the partial exemption calculation where appropriate (Trading Funds only) – end of financial year.

Updates & Information – the plan should include regular scheduled updates – advising of any significant changes with GD implications – quarterly or end of financial year.

VAT & GOVERNMENT DEPARTMENTS

3   Contracted-Out Services

3.1   Contracted-Out Services (COS)

COS is a Treasury refund mechanism of the amount of the VAT incurred on eligible services under VAT Act 1994 s.41(3). It is a form of funding and, theoretically, HM Treasury budgets for amounts recoverable as COS in funding GDs and the NHS. HMRC administers COS recovery on behalf of the Treasury. It is important to reiterate that COS refunds are outside the scope of VAT and are not tax, specifically not input tax (i.e. there is no entitlement in tax law to receive the refund) and there is no overlap between the s.41 special legal regime and the VAT regime. The VAT regime is governed by UK law giving indirect effect to EU law whereas the COS regime is a compensation scheme arising from public policy in UK law (and subordinate to EU law).

There are currently seven similar compensation schemes in the 28 Member States of the EU (*VAT in the Public Sector and Exemptions in the Public Interest* TAXUD/2009/DE/316) including Austria, Denmark, Finland, France, Portugal, Spain and Sweden (eight in total including the UK). There are also other versions of VAT public sector compensation schemes outside the EU, notably in Canada, Australia and New Zealand.

3.1.1   Background

COS was introduced in 1983 as a result of government policy to open up the public sector to private sector competition in various areas of activity. Private sector organisations charging VAT for their services would have been at a competitive disadvantage against internal public sector providers which did not. GDs and the NHS were encouraged to contract-out services to the private sector which would have traditionally been performed in-house. It was recognised that many of these services would be subject to VAT and where they were acquired for 'non-business' purposes, the non-reclaimable VAT could act as a disincentive to contracting-out. The solution was to refund the VAT incurred on the charges by the private sector providers but only in limited areas and only for services (although s.41(3) actually refers to "goods or services").

It was decided to compensate GDs (and the NHS) by a direct refund mechanism, which is now provided for in section 41(3) of the VAT Act 1994. Under this provision, the Treasury issues Directions, commonly known as the 'Contracting-Out Directions' which lists both the GDs and NHS organisations eligible to claim refunds of VAT, and the services on which VAT can be refunded. The most recent Treasury Directions date from 2 December 2002 (see **Appendix 2** and **Appendix 3**) although a current revision is pending. It contains a List of Eligible Services (see **Appendix 4**), a List of Business Activities (see **Appendix 5**) and a List of Eligible Departments (see **Appendix 6**). Treasury Directions are regularly published in the London, Edinburgh and Belfast Gazettes and the pending revisions will not take effect until published in the Gazettes.

3.1.2   VAT Act 1994 Section 41

Section 41(3) provides:

(3) Where VAT is chargeable on the supply of goods or services to a Government department, on the acquisition of any goods by a Government department from another Member State or on the importation of any goods by a Government department from a place outside the Member States and the supply, acquisition or importation is not for the purpose—

(a) of any business carried on by the department, or

(b) of a supply by the department which, by virtue of section 41A, is treated as a supply in the course or furtherance of a business, then, if and to the extent that the Treasury so direct and subject to subsection (4) below, the Commissioners shall, on a claim made by the department at such time and in such form and manner as the Commissioners may determine, refund to it the amount of the VAT so chargeable.

(Reproduced in full at **Appendix 1**)

There are four conditions for eligibility for COS recovery:
(1) the services are listed in the Treasury Refund Directions;
(2) the services are not for a business purpose;
(3) the historical capability to perform the service in-house existed anywhere within government or the NHS (anywhere within government rather within an individual GD); and
(4) the claim must be made within four months of the end of the relevant financial year i.e. by 31 July (previously 30 June) following the 31 March each year.

All of the conditions must be satisfied before an amount of VAT charged can be reclaimed as COS.

3.1.3   Public sector exemption

The European Commission is currently undertaking a review into the operation of VAT in the public sector across the EU and in OECD countries outside the EU. Eight EU countries (including the UK) operate public policy compensation schemes (i.e. refunds under s.33, s.41 and s.99 in the UK) The initial EC conclusion was that the differential treatment between public and private sector activities causes a distortion of competition contrary to EU law and considers various options to eliminate this distortion which it found reduced economic efficiency and welfare (because the compensation schemes are not tax and fall outside the terms of the Principal VAT Directive it would be impossible to standardise them under the tax harmonisation provisions).

The distortion takes two forms: first, there may be an effect on inputs as there will be a reduced incentive for the public sector to outsource support services/back office-services, such as cleaning services, IT services, accountancy and facility management etc; and secondly, there may be an effect on outputs through the reduced competitiveness of the private sector in comparison with the public sector. One option would be to extend a refund scheme similar to s.33 or s.41 to all 28 Member States but the EC notes that this would only remedy the first distortion on inputs. One proposed solution is full taxation, removing the public policy compensation schemes completely (including s.33, s.41 and s.99) and thus remedying both the first and second distortions.

An EU wide consultation was undertaken in 2014 and the public sector exemption via a public policy compensation scheme such as COS is still under review.

3.1.4   Recent developments

The Treasury has agreed that COS refunds may be claimed for the following activities which will be included in the next revision of the Directions:

(1) Call centre and contact centre services
(2) Services provided through International Trade Advisers for UK Trade and Investment
(3) Services provided under Framework for Procuring External Support for Commissioners (FESC) other than:
  - supplies of computer services and professional services that are excluded from the scope of Headings 14 and 52 above, unless the Treasury directs otherwise, and
  - elsewhere, the supply of staff.

At date of publication certain headings are not included in the HMRC Manual VATGPB9700 because they are currently being drafted for the online manual; for these headings HMRC advise that the current guidance notes should be used as these remain extant until the revised and updated version is published in the online manual. The latest guidance notes issued by HMRC for GDs was in 2012 (*Guidance Notes for Government Departments* Seventh Edition Issued: 19 July 2012).

Budget March 2015

It was announced that eligibility for COS refunds was to be extended to NDPBs operating in a shared service context. When implemented this measure will effectively extend the COS relief available to the NHS and GDs in relation to non-business activities to NDPBs (and possibly other organisations) operating in a shared service context. Previously, NDPBs have had no special VAT relief and the VAT incurred has been an irrecoverable cost (partial exemption still applies).

The overall policy is for public bodies to enter into shared services arrangements. Where this happens the body or bodies providing services to the others engages in a business activity for VAT purposes, just as any supplier of this type of service does, and VAT is charged to the purchasers of the services. To date these services have mainly been in the fields of HR, recruitment and training, and IT services. There has been no provision to refund VAT to NDPBs sharing services with their parent GD or between themselves. With the expected wider take-up of shared services, the Government wishes to ensure that these bodies are not at a VAT disadvantage when they enter into such arrangements. Because of competition issues, this will also include situations where they procure an eligible service directly from a private sector provider.

A proposed new section 33E of the VAT Act 1994 (currently deferred) will allow the refund of VAT incurred by named bodies on services purchased for their non-business purposes. Before a body can be named, it (or its parent GD) must have entered into an agreement with HM Treasury to adjust the overall level of its public funding to take into account the VAT that will be recoverable. This is because such funding includes tax liabilities.

Because it will not be possible to name bodies in primary legislation as and when such agreements are made with the Treasury the measure contains a power to make Treasury Orders to name the bodies. While it is expected that most bodies will be NDPBs the extension will not be limited to them as there are other types of arms-length public body that may qualify. The Treasury consider it appropriate for these bodies to have the same level of VAT recovery as is available to GDs under COS. Consequently, the Treasury (Contracting-Out) Directions which lists the eligible services upon which VAT can be recovered is also the direction made for the same purpose under this measure.

3.1.5 Contracted-out

COS Headings relate by definition to the provision of a specific service by an external contractor or supplier (i.e. contracted-out) rather than to costs incurred by a GD in procuring the service for itself (although if services these may be recoverable under another COS Heading). This is fundamental: the service must be contracted-out to be eligible for recovery.

3.1.6 Exempt business activities

COS recovery is not allowed in relation to exempt business activities. For GDs if an eligible service is partly attributable to an exempt business activity then it is not recoverable.

3.1.7 Leasing or hire of equipment

Recovery on leasing or hire of equipment is only allowed under Headings 25 and 26 in relation to photocopiers or reprographic equipment or vehicles on the condition that the hire or leasing includes repair and maintenance. Any other leasing or hire of equipment is not recoverable. There is a partial exception to this under Heading 14 which allows recovery on the hire or rental of certain data land lines and private data circuits but not on equipment as such. Recovery on repair and maintenance included in a leasing contract is not allowed even where there is a separate contract unless there is no bar to the repair and maintenance being supplied by another provider in which case it is recoverable.

3.1.8 Agency staff

Recovery on agency staff hire is not allowed except in relation to nurses or auxiliaries under Heading 41 – Nursing services (which may be exempt by concession in any case). Typical areas where recovery is not allowed is agency IT, finance and professional staff however there is a distinction between a supply of staff and a supply of services and it is advisable to analyse the nature of the supply because the charging mechanism for a staff agency or service company may be similar e.g. based on hours/days on site. A potentially eligible contract for services will mean that the service company controls the staff and has responsibility (and liability) for the performance of the service; otherwise the supply is likely to be one of staff and ineligible for recovery.

3.1.9 Minor COS headings

Several of the COS Headings are of negligible importance (e.g. ceremonial services) or relate to primarily to exempt supplies (i.e. where VAT will not or should not be charged by the supplier). These include nursing services, childcare services and welfare services.

3.1.10 Managed services

A managed service contract is one where an external contractor or supplier provides an eligible service on a managed basis usually including equipment or goods which would not be recoverable in its own right but the cost of which is included in the provision of the eligible service. Generally, the gross cost of a managed service is higher than the constituent elements (to reflect the management cost) but with COS recovery the net cost is often lower and may be more cost effective overall. HMRC usually accept these in relation to administrative functions and technology e.g. IT and telephone systems, admin/records etc provided the service which is managed actually falls under a COS Heading (it is not enough that it is a service, it must be an eligible service). Where equipment is operated by the supplier's staff as part of the managed service contract the likelihood of approval for recovery is increased.

3.1.11   Repair and maintenance

COS recovery is allowed on repair and maintenance on a range of activities e.g. the maintenance and non-structural repair of buildings (where funded from revenue expenditure), the maintenance and repair of civil engineering works (where funded from revenue expenditure, and the maintenance and repair of vehicles, plant, and equipment). Repair and maintenance means the reinstatement of the repaired item to its original state, and it therefore excludes any new work or new build construction. It includes the use of different or better materials where the original materials are obsolete and also incidental supplies of goods such as parts for vehicles, plant or equipment. Recovery is allowed on parts included under a repair and maintenance contract or where these are supplied as part of an ad hoc service. Recovery is not allowed on the installation of plant or equipment, nor on the replacement of a whole item of plant or equipment but is allowed on the repair by replacement of parts or components.

The repair and maintenance of buildings (including refurbishment and cleaning) is allowed under COS Heading 35 but not new work (e.g. additions or alterations) or new build construction, extensions, installations or improvements (including preventive maintenance which improves the building) or work which is funded from capital expenditure (only from revenue expenditure). Routine and backlog maintenance are recoverable and replacement of an eligible item would also be considered to be repairs and maintenance as long as that item is reinstated in the same location. Equally, any materials used would be considered to be an integral part of the service.

3.1.12   Incidental supplies

VAT charged on goods supplied incidental to a service is also recoverable as COS e.g. parts supplied as part of a repair or maintenance service such as vehicle repairs or maintenance. To qualify for recovery on incidental goods the principal supply must be one of eligible services and all VAT charged is therefore recoverable as COS. Correspondingly, there is no COS recovery in relation to the corollary, a supply of services incidental to a principal supply of goods e.g. a maintenance service provided as part of a contract for the supply of equipment.

3.1.13 COS time limits

According to Treasury policy COS must be claimed within four months (previously three months) of the end of the financial year i.e. 31 July following 31 March (occasionally varied to take account of weekends etc, but otherwise a rigidly observed deadline) in order to preserve fiscal certainty in the public finances, that is, to ensure that there are no retrospective adjustments which would affect annual budgets. Until 1997 retrospective claims for up to six years could be made but, in line with a general tightening of the VAT regime in response to Kenneth Clarke's "black hole" in Treasury VAT revenues (e.g. the introduction of the capping provisions in 1996/97), this was changed to the current financial year. Fiscal certainty applies equally to overclaims and underclaims of COS and in accordance with Treasury policy any adjustment (whether of overclaims or underclaims) must be made no later than the 31 July (plus 7 days for online filing) following the end of the financial year on 31 March (i.e. in the June VAT Return due by 31 July).

3.1.14 VAT returns

HMRC have authority under VAT Act 1994 s.41 to determine the time, form and manner of claims and the Commissioners have determined that COS claims or adjustments must be made in an online VAT Return (although this is an administrative practice only – s.41 refunds are not technically part of a VAT Return). This means that it is not possible to make last minute submissions by email or error correction notification to HMRC Offices. This also means that in practice the June VAT return (due by the following 31 July) is the last Return in which an adjustment for the previous financial year (April – March) can be included. In exceptional circumstances it is possible to seek permission from HMRC to render an estimated July Return early i.e. by 31 July (rather than by 31 August when due) to avoid a potential loss of COS entitlement (*VAT Regulations 28 & 29(3) SI 1995/2518*).

3.1.15 Correction of COS errors

The correction of a COS error is now treated as an error on a VAT Return and, at the discretion of the Commissioners on an administrative basis, is subject to the normal rules on ECNs (albeit that technically ECNs only apply to errors within the scope of the tax i.e. VAT errors (*VAT Notice 700/45/10*)). If under the ECN limits COS adjustments should be included in the current VAT 21 for inclusion in the current VAT Return but otherwise must be notified to the Government Departments Team.

3.1.16 Retention of records

All records and supporting documentation relating to a refund of VAT on contracted-out services, including tax invoices, must be retained for a period of six years from the date the claim is made. Invoices may be scanned or transferred onto microfilm or microfiche, provided that copies can be easily produced and that there are adequate facilities for allowing HMRC to view them when required. Microfilm or microfiche records must also be kept for a period of six years from the date the claim is made. The six year retention period for COS records parallels the requirement to retain VAT records for six years (*VAT Act 1994 Schedule 11 para 6(3)*). The agreement of HMRC must be obtained if records are to be destroyed within the six year period (except where these are converted into electronic format).

3.2   COS Headings 1-76

1 - Accounting, invoicing and related services

This Heading concerns the outsourcing of all, or part, of an accounts department although it also covers the procurement of the type of services which would have been undertaken by an accounts department. The exclusions are functions which either had to be procured from external accountants or have since evolved as services supplied by external accountants. It would not include VAT incurred on external audit fees as, by their very nature, they would never have been performed in-house so could not be contracted out.

It includes any accounting or accountancy service performed by an external contractor or supplier, or any service in relation to invoicing or the preparation, processing or sending of invoices.

- Accounting – includes the preparation of any type of financial accounts, statements or reports, bookkeeping or general financial record keeping.
- Invoicing – includes the preparation, processing or sending of invoices (by an external contractor or supplier).
- Tax Returns – includes the preparation of tax returns (but see below in relation to tax planning etc).

It excludes the services of external auditors in preparing audited annual accounts on the basis that a statutory audit by definition cannot be performed in-house. Only the statutory element of services provided by external auditors is ineligible. Other services such as value for money audits are eligible for recovery but the hire of accountants or tax advisers to carry out tax health checks or tax planning advice is specifically excluded. Other accounting services which by definition must be provided externally e.g. for regulatory purposes are not recoverable.

Notes – internal audit reports dealing with efficiency etc and advisory services such as management or financial consultancy are also currently eligible for recovery under Heading 52. The storage of financial records or invoices is recoverable under COS Heading 63.

References – HMRC VAT Manual VATGPB9750 (24 March 2015)

http://www.hmrc.gov.uk/manuals/vatgpbmanual/VATGPB9750.htm

2 - Administration of the following: Career development loans, Certificates of Experience, Government support payments to the Railway Industry Pension Funds, Grants and awards, Services supplied under the Companies Acts and the Patent and Trademarks Acts, Teachers' Superannuation Scheme, Vehicle Excise Duty refunds, Winter fuel payment scheme, Inherited State Earnings Related Pension Scheme, Student Loan Scheme, Fast Track Teaching Programme

This includes the administration by an external contractor or supplier of the following:

- Career Development Loans
- Certificates of Experience
- Government support payments to the Railway Industry Pensions Funds
- Grants and Awards
- Services supplied under the Companies Acts and the Patents and Trademark Acts
- Teacher's Superannuation Scheme
- Vehicle Excise Duty Refunds
- Winter Fuel Payment Scheme
- Inherited State Earnings Related Pension Scheme
- Student Loan Scheme
- Fast Track Teaching Programme

It excludes services other than those relating to the named programmes. New programmes can only be added to the list with the agreement of the Treasury.

References – HMRC VAT Manual VATGPB9770 (24 March 2015)

http://www.hmrc.gov.uk/manuals/vatgpbmanual/VATGPB9770.htm

3 - Administration and collection of toll charges

This includes the administration and collection of toll charges by an external contractor or supplier.

References – HMRC VAT Manual VATGPB9790 (24 March 2015)

http://www.hmrc.gov.uk/manuals/vatgpbmanual/VATGPB9790.htm

4 - Aerial photographic surveys and aerial surveillance

This includes the carrying out of aerial photographic surveys or surveillance by an external contractor or supplier (including satellite imagery and photographs).

References – HMRC VAT Manual VATGPB9810 (24 March 2015)

http://www.hmrc.gov.uk/manuals/vatgpbmanual/VATGPB9810.htm

5 - Agricultural services of the kind normally carried out by the Farming and Rural Conservation Agency

This includes the provision of agricultural services of the kind normally carried out by DEFRA by an external contractor or supplier or agricultural services of the kind normally carried out by the Farming and Rural Conservation Agency.

The wording of this Heading was amended in 2008 when the Farming and Rural Conservation Agency was abolished.

The Heading can be used by the relevant departments of the devolved administrations which have assumed responsibility for such activities from DEFRA.

References – HMRC VAT Manual VATGPB9830 (24 March 2015)

http://www.hmrc.gov.uk/manuals/vatgpbmanual/VATGPB9830.htm

6 - Alteration, repair and maintenance of road schemes, except (a) any works carried out pursuant to an agreement made under section 278 of the Highways Act 1980, or (b) works involving construction on land not already used for road schemes

This includes any service performed by an external contractor or supplier which may be reasonably construed as the alteration, repair or maintenance of an existing road.

Alterations – alterations to roads including the cost of materials and equipment (including hire) where this is part of a single (or composite) supply of services (and incidental to the supply of the services). Includes changing the layout of existing roads e.g. for the purposes of access or improvement.

Repair – repair of roads including the cost of materials and equipment (including hire) where this is part of a single (or composite) supply of services (and incidental to the supply of the services).

Maintenance – maintenance of roads including the cost of materials and equipment (including hire) where this is part of a single (or composite) supply of services (and incidental to the supply of the service).

It excludes new road construction (even for the purposes of access, the work cannot be new construction). Also excludes work pursuant to an agreement under Highways Act 1980 s.278 (which allows Highways Authorities to enter into agreements with private developers or third parties to pay for or carry out work in relation to public highways). Also excludes the gritting of roads in severe weather (revised from the previous guidance).

Notes – excludes materials, goods and the hire or purchase of equipment except where these are part of a single (or composite) supply of services and incidental to the supply of the services i.e. materials, goods or the hire or purchase of equipment purchased separately is ineligible for recovery.

Section 278 Agreements

Section 278 of the Highways Act 1980 allows a Highways Authority (HA) to seek contributions from developers towards the cost of works considered to be for the "common good". For example, these works could include the construction of a new slip road or roundabout.

Any work carried out by an HA under a section 278 agreement is a non-business activity for VAT purposes. This is because the HA has a statutory responsibility under the Highways Act 1980, to maintain the road on which the work is carried out. As such, the construction works form part of the HA's statutory responsibilities for maintaining the road.

Heading 6 of the Treasury's Contracting-Out Directions prevents GDs from recovering VAT they incur when undertaking works under section 278 agreements. The heading is entitled "Alteration, repair and maintenance of road schemes, except (a) any works carried out pursuant to an agreement made under section 278 of the Highways Act 1980"

As the HA is not able to claim a refund of the VAT under section 41(3) of the VAT Act 1994, it is a condition of the Section 278 agreement that the contributions they receive include irrecoverable VAT.

The HA cannot issue a VAT invoice to the bodies making contributions because it is seeking a reimbursement of costs and not making a supply. The contributor will be unable to recover any VAT element included in the contribution they pay to the HA. This is because the VAT amount does not relate to a supply, which has been made to the contributor. The contractor carrying out the works will always be making a supply to the HA.

Hybrid Road Schemes

"Hybrid Road Schemes" are works comprised of new construction together with improvements to the existing road schemes.

As the hybrid schemes involve two types of work, new construction and alteration, the costs must be separately identified for VAT purposes. This is because some of the VAT incurred on new construction undertaken in the hybrid scheme cannot be recovered.

It can sometimes prove difficult to separate the actual expenditure on new construction from that on alteration etc. HMRC allows an apportionment of costs to be made based on the terms of the additional contract.

In cases where it is not possible to directly attribute VAT elements, apportionment may be allowed. Hybrid road schemes are an example of a situation where permission to apportion the VAT has been granted.

References – HMRC VAT Manual VATGPB9850 (24 March 2015)

http://www.hmrc.gov.uk/manuals/vatgpbmanual/VATGPB9850.htm

7 - Broadcast monitoring services

This includes the provision of broadcast monitoring services by an external contractor or supplier such as:

- recording news and TV programmes which are relevant to the work of a GD;
- recording radio programmes
- providing a digest of a departments coverage in the broadcast media
- social media monitoring e.g. Facebook, Twitter etc.

References – HMRC VAT Manual VATGPB9870 (24 March 2015)

http://www.hmrc.gov.uk/manuals/vatgpbmanual/VATGPB9870.htm

8 - Cartographic services

This includes the provision of mapping or cartographic services by an external contractor or supplier such as:

- mapping services
- topographical surveys
- preparation of customised maps.

References – HMRC VAT Manual VATGPB9890 (24 March 2015)

http://www.hmrc.gov.uk/manuals/vatgpbmanual/VATGPB9890.htm

9 - Cash in transit services

This includes any service performed by an external contractor or supplier providing cash in transit services for the safe or secure transport of cash or monies, including wage packeting case deliveries and associated equipment. Also includes the provision of security guards or secure vehicles for the safe or secure transport of cash or monies as part of a single (or composite) supply of services and incidental to the supply of the services.

It excludes supply or provision of security equipment or vehicles per se (including lease or hire).

Notes – the repair or maintenance of security equipment is recoverable under Heading 37 and the provision of security guards for purposes other than the safe or secure transport of monies is recoverable under Heading 60.

References – HMRC VAT Manual VATGPB9910 (24 March 2015)

http://www.hmrc.gov.uk/manuals/vatgpbmanual/VATGPB9910.htm

10 - Catering

This includes the supply or provision of catering services by an external contractor or supplier (either in running a GD catering function or in relation to individual events) such as food prepared and facilities supplied by a contract catering service and:

- catering services for occasional functions
- services associated with catering for occasional functions which form part of the supply of catering e.g. staff to serve food and drink, serving alcoholic beverages, hire of additional equipment (mobile kitchens, etc) to supplement the on-site facilities
- vending machines when supplied as part of a catering contract
- catering services for official functions e.g. receptions, dinners and banquets.

It excludes the purchases of food or drink and sandwich or food delivery services.

Catering – a supply of catering is a supply of food which incorporates a significant element of service. The purchase of pre-packed food or retail food for patients or meetings e.g. sandwiches or snacks, would not be viewed as catering because there is no significant element of service in the supply, rather it would be viewed as a supply of goods. However, if the sandwiches or snacks are specifically prepared to order then that would qualify as catering.

Notes – the supply or provision of catering services to staff or visitors for a consideration or charge is taxable.

References – HMRC VAT Manual VATGPB9930 (24 March 2015)

http://www.hmrc.gov.uk/manuals/vatgpbmanual/VATGPB9930.htm

11 - Ceremonial services

This includes the provision of ceremonial or event management services by an external contractor or supplier such as:

- erecting seating and stands for dignitaries and the general public
- putting up flags and bunting
- hire of portable toilet facilities
- putting up and dismantling crowd control barriers
- hire of p.a. systems
- laying the "red carpet"

It excludes recovery on purchases of goods, for example:

- flags
- flowers
- red carpet
- food or drink for hospitality purposes
- fireworks that are to be used in a display

Notes – ceremonial services takes its everyday meaning e.g. opening new public buildings etc or hospital wing.

References – HMRC VAT Manual VATGPB9950 (24 March 2015)

http://www.hmrc.gov.uk/manuals/vatgpbmanual/VATGPB9950.htm

12 - Childcare services

This includes the provision of childcare or crèche/nursery services (including holiday play schemes) by an external contractor or supplier where the supply is for the benefit of the GDs own employees.

It excludes the admin fee on childcare vouchers.

Notes – the provision of childcare or crèche/nursery services in the course or furtherance of business and where the supplier is registered with OFSTED (under the Children Act 1989 as amended by the Care Standards Act 2000) is exempt under VATA 94 Schedule 9 Group 7 Item 9.

Supplies of childcare or crèche/nursery services by an eligible educational body are also exempt under VATA 94 Schedule 9 Group 6 Item 1.

Supplies of childcare or crèche/nursery services by a charity where charges are designed only to cover costs is outside the scope of VAT.

In principle, the service is otherwise standard-rated but exemptions from OFSTED registration are rare and it is unlikely that VAT would be charged on this service (or that a GD would engage a supplier not registered by OFSTED). COS recovery on the agency admin fee on childcare vouchers (taxable) is not allowed by HMRC.

References – HMRC VAT Manual VATGPB9970 (24 March 2015)

http://www.hmrc.gov.uk/manuals/vatgpbmanual/VATGPB9970.htm

13 - Collection, delivery and distribution services

This includes the provision by an external contractor or supplier of any form of collection, delivery, distribution (or storage) service, regardless of the nature of the items involved e.g. goods, packages or documents via internal distribution, courier services or carriage charges (separate from a supply of goods). Essentially, if a GD orders a specific collection or delivery (separate from a supply of goods) then that would be recoverable. Also includes Royal Mail services where subject to VAT (historically exempt).

It excludes delivery charges as part of a supply of goods even where separately itemised on an Invoice. This would be part of a single (or composite) supply of delivered goods rather than an eligible service. Essentially, if a manufacturer or supplier includes a delivery charge as part of the purchase price this would not be recoverable.

References – HMRC VAT Manual VATGPB9990 (24 March 2015)

http://www.hmrc.gov.uk/manuals/vatgpbmanual/VATGPB9990.htm

14 - Computer services supplied to the specification of the recipient including:

- *the provision by one or more suppliers of a fully managed and serviced computer infrastructure either using the recipients' own hardware or hardware provided by the supplier as part of the infrastructure; and*
- *the development, delivery and support of bespoke software.*

Excluding:
- *supply and support of off-the-shelf software;*
- *hire of hardware alone;*
- *line rental alone;*
- *telephony; and*
- *hire of computer consultants to add expertise to in-house IT teams.*

This includes computer services supplied to the specification of the recipient including: the provision by one or more suppliers of a fully managed and serviced computer infrastructure either using the recipients' own hardware or hardware provided by the supplier as part of the infrastructure; and the development, delivery and support of bespoke software. It specifically includes data services and also the hire of computer link-up services, the hire of land lines used to link up computers and the hire of private circuits to link up computers in different geographic locations, and also includes fully managed services and the provision of outsourced computerised payroll services or data processing services outsourced to an external contractor or supplier.

Bespoke Software – software which has been ordered, designed and created to the specification of the recipient. It does not include the development of additional software in relation to an off-the-shelf product, or software licences, software packages designed for general use by GDs, off-the-shelf software packages, or software packages specially designed for a third party. Typically, an all-inclusive charge on the same Invoice may be made for the supply of computer services (and/or hardware) including services on which, if supplied separately, VAT incurred on costs would be eligible for COS recovery (e.g. software maintenance, or professional services such as computer consultancy work, including contract software development, which could include modification and adaptation to existing software packages). Where there is a mixed (or multiple supply) the recoverable elements may be extracted and claimed. A multiple (or mixed) supply means that the eligible services would be capable of being separately ordered, negotiated or contracted and are not incidental to a principal supply of goods or ineligible services.

It excludes the supply and support of off-the-shelf software (support included as part of an off-the-shelf package would be part of a single (or composite) supply of goods), the hire or purchase of computer hardware of itself, line rental of itself; telephony, and the hire of computer consultants to add expertise to in-house IT teams (or the use of agency professional IT consultants). Specifically excludes voice services and also the leasing of networked computer systems, the rental of telephone appliances and lines, pager rentals, or car radio rental, telephone line rental in connection with computer systems. Also excludes the installation of computers or equipment of itself, connection charges and management and/or maintenance of a provider's lines.

Notes – maintenance of computer hardware is eligible for recovery under COS Heading 37. This Heading was revised in 2007 (see below):

Heading 14: The purpose of the direction, as you are aware, is to refund VAT incurred on services at one time performed in-house and now increasingly contracted-out, rather than on services that have always been purchased from the private sector. Information technology [IT] is an area where there are constant changes is technology and the services purchased by departments are becoming increasingly removed from the IT services once performed in house. More significantly for the direction the methods of procuring these services are changing. The revised direction therefore replaces "Computer services supplied to the specification of the recipient, including the provision of a fully managed and serviced computer infrastructure" with:

"Computer services supplied to the specification of the recipient including:

the provision by one or more suppliers of a fully managed and serviced computer infrastructure either using the recipients' own hardware or hardware provided by the supplier as part of the infrastructure; and the development, delivery and support of bespoke software.

Excluding:
- supply and support of off-the-shelf software;
- hire of hardware alone;
- line rental alone;
- telephony; and
- hire of computer consultants to add expertise to in-house IT teams."

It is hoped that this new wording makes more explicit what services and procurement arrangements are covered and the sort of services that are not. Previously the scope of the heading reflected the PFI type procurements common in IT where the infrastructure had to be provided by a single provider on hardware owned by the provider. Treasury have recognised that the use of single providers is no longer viewed as always giving the best service and that for security and continuity reasons departments may wish to retain ownership of the hardware (even though under a PFI arrangement this decreases the transfer of risk from the department). Treasury Ministers have agreed that departments may recover VAT incurred on heading 14 services under this revised heading from 1st April 2006.

References – HMRC Circular Letter 27/03/07/p47 *Guidance Notes for Government Departments* Seventh Edition Issued: 19 July 2012.

15 - *Conference and exhibition services*

This includes the supply of a compound package of conference or exhibition services or facilities by an external contractor or supplier e.g. from a hotel or conference centre, including accommodation, meals, room hire etc. for a conference in relation to the non-business activities of a GD.

Conference – a planned large scale organised event usually attended by external delegates.

Exhibition – exhibition services include the provision of event management services by an external contractor or supplier e.g. audio visual services, event display and presentation services or the provision of reception and event staff as part of a single (or composite) supply of event management services.

It excludes the provision of accommodation per se by a hotel without the compound conference facilities (even if described as a "conference" or "delegate" rate) or the provision of meeting room hire of itself. There must be a supply of more than just accommodation and catering, the GD must receive a compound package e.g. the services of staff, room, equipment and catering etc.

Notes – if a GD holds a conference or meeting for which a charge is made to delegates and the conference or meeting does not relate to the non-business activities of the GD this could be an exempt supply because any conferencing or training (i.e. CPD) event held by a GD (as an "eligible body") would be exempt under VAT Act 1994 Schedule 9 Group 6 and therefore any VAT incurred on costs would not be eligible for COS recovery. If the conference or meeting falls outside the definition of training or professional development then it would be a taxable supply and there would be input tax entitlement (but output tax would be chargeable).

References – HMRC VAT Manual VATGPB10030 (24 March 2015)

http://www.hmrc.gov.uk/manuals/vatgpbmanual/VATGPB10030.htm

16 - Debt collection

This includes the provision of debt collection services by an external contractor or supplier e.g. by a professional debt collection agency, legal firm or bailiff services (revised from the previous guidance).

References – HMRC VAT Manual VATGPB10050 (24 March 2015)

http://www.hmrc.gov.uk/manuals/vatgpbmanual/VATGPB10050.htm

17 - Departmental staff records and payroll systems including administration and payment of pensions

This includes the provision of services by an external contractor or supplier to deal with departmental staff records and payroll systems or the administration or payment of pensions. Also actuarial services in respect of pensions, supplies by civil service pensions or similar bodies, or services supplied by government actuarial departments.

It excludes the administration of child care vouchers.

References – HMRC VAT Manual VATGPB10070 (24 March 2015)

http://www.hmrc.gov.uk/manuals/vatgpbmanual/VATGPB10070.htm

18 - *Employment advisory services as directed by the Race Relations Act 1976*

This includes the provision of employment advisory services as directed by the Equality Act 2010 by an external contractor or supplier including supplies by civil service policy (the Race Relations Act 1976 has been repealed).

References – HMRC VAT Manual VATGPB10090 (24 March 2015)

http://www.hmrc.gov.uk/manuals/vatgpbmanual/VATGPB10090.htm

19 - *Engineering and related process services*

This includes the provision of engineering and related process services by an external contractor or supplier, specifically in relation to manufacturing and the related commissioning processes.

It excludes the installation of plant and computer engineering.

References – HMRC VAT Manual VATGPB10110 (24 March 2015)

http://www.hmrc.gov.uk/manuals/vatgpbmanual/VATGPB10110.htm

20 - *Environmental protection services of the kind normally carried out for the Department of the Environment, Food and Rural Affairs*

This includes the provision of services by an external contractor or supplier in relation to environmental protection services of the kind normally carried out for the Department for Environment, Food and Rural Affairs (DEFRA).

References – HMRC VAT Manual VATGPB10130 (24 March 2015)

http://www.hmrc.gov.uk/manuals/vatgpbmanual/VATGPB10130.htm

21 - *Estate management services*

This includes the provision by an external contractor or supplier of estate management services such as a facilities management service or the management of a building complex, including arranging for the payment of rents or other charges, dealing with repairs and maintenance, arranging cleaning, security, post etc. The service would be a management service rather than the direct provision of specific services which are otherwise recoverable under COS Heading 35 (repairs, maintenance, cleaning) or COS Heading 60 (security). It may also include utilities and equipment costs where these are part of a single (composite) supply or unitary charge.

It excludes separate recharges of utilities (supplies of goods).

Applies where a GD holds either the leasehold or the freehold on the property (or the equivalent under the law of Scotland).

References – HMRC VAT Manual VATGPB10150 (24 March 2015)

http://www.hmrc.gov.uk/manuals/vatgpbmanual/VATGPB10150.htm

22 - *Export intelligence services*

This includes the provision of export intelligence services by an external contractor or supplier.

References – HMRC VAT Manual VATGPB10170 (24 March 2015)

http://www.hmrc.gov.uk/manuals/vatgpbmanual/VATGPB10170.htm

23 - *Filming, audio-visual and production services*

This includes the provision of filming, audio-visual and production services by an external contractor or supplier for in-house training films, promotional videos for public awareness campaigns or filming or recording briefings, meetings or conferences etc.

References – HMRC VAT Manual VATGPB10190 (24 March 2015)

http://www.hmrc.gov.uk/manuals/vatgpbmanual/VATGPB10190.htm

24 - *Health promotion activities*

This includes the provision by an external contractor or supplier of health promotional activities, such as a health promotion campaign or health promotion advertisements.

It excludes VAT on costs incurred directly by an NHS organisation in carrying on health promotion activities itself unless these are otherwise eligible for recovery under another heading (e.g. the direct placement of health promotion advertisements is not eligible for recovery).

References – HMRC VAT Manual VATGPB10210 (24 March 2015)

http://www.hmrc.gov.uk/manuals/vatgpbmanual/VATGPB10210.htm

25 - *Hire of reprographic equipment including repair and maintenance.*

This includes the hire of reprographic equipment where the rental agreement/contract includes repairs and maintenance. Also includes hires where the charge or maintenance element of the agreement/contract is calculated on a "copy charge" basis. Also parts supplied and fitted as part of the maintenance element of the agreement/contract.

It excludes the hire of reprographic equipment where the rental agreement/contract does not include repairs and maintenance, the hire of fax machines and the purchase of consumables such as toner or copy paper.

References – p49 *Guidance Notes for Government Departments* Seventh Edition Issued: 19 July 2012.

26 - *Hire of vehicles, including repair and maintenance*

This includes the contract hire of cars or commercial vehicles that come under the classification of operating leases where repair and maintenance is supplied as part of the leasing agreement/contract e.g. individual vehicles or pool cars.

It excludes the contract hire of cars or commercial vehicles that come under the classification of operating leases where repair and maintenance is not supplied as part of the leasing agreement/contract. From 1 April 2004 VAT incurred on costs is not eligible for COS recovery under this category where the repair and maintenance of the vehicles is carried out by another GD. Also excludes short term car hire. The definition of "short term" is whether the vehicle would be substituted or repaired on breakdown. For short term car hire the vehicle would normally be substituted but on a contract hire or leasing arrangement the vehicle would be repaired. Also excludes the short term hire of commercial vehicles or plant.

References – p49 *Guidance Notes for Government Departments* Seventh Edition Issued: 19 July 2012.

27 - *Insolvency services*

This includes the provision by an external contractor or supplier of insolvency services but only where it can be demonstrated that the insolvency practitioners are working under contract to a GD and that their services are being provided to the GD. In many cases insolvency practitioners provide their services to the business under their supervision and therefore the supply is to that business.

References – HMRC VAT Manual VATGPB10270 (24 March 2015)

http://www.hmrc.gov.uk/manuals/vatgpbmanual/VATGPB10270.htm

28 - *Interpretation and translation services*

This includes the services of an interpreter or translator or the provision by an external contractor or supplier of interpretation or translation services such as simultaneous translation or interpretation services provided in person at events or meetings or via telephone or the translation of documents. Also includes sign language services.

References – HMRC VAT Manual VATGPB10290 (24 March 2015)

http://www.hmrc.gov.uk/manuals/vatgpbmanual/VATGPB10290.htm

29 - *Issue of documents to, and control of, bingo halls and off-course bookmakers*

This includes the services of issuing documents to, and control of, bingo halls and off-course bookmakers by an external contractor or supplier.

References – HMRC VAT Manual VATGPB10310 (24 March 2015)

http://www.hmrc.gov.uk/manuals/vatgpbmanual/VATGPB10310.htm

30 - *Issue of documents under Wireless and Telegraphy Act*

This includes the services of issuing documents under the Wireless Telegraphy Act by an external contractor or supplier.

References – HMRC VAT Manual VATGPB10330 (24 March 2015)

http://www.hmrc.gov.uk/manuals/vatgpbmanual/VATGPB10330.htm

31 - *Laboratory services*

This includes the provision by an external contractor or supplier of laboratory services such as the analysis of samples, drug testing or forensic testing.

It excludes the provision of laboratory consumables such as reagents, chemicals, test tubes.

References – p50 *Guidance Notes for Government Departments* Seventh Edition Issued: 19 July 2012.

32 - *Laundry services*

This includes the cleaning or laundering of clothing, linen and fabrics by an external contractor or supplier. Also, dry cleaning services, towel hire, towel cleaning services and the provision and exchange of linen on a regular basis for laundering (which remains the property of the company providing the service). Also, the cleaning and laundering of uniforms and fabrics.

It excludes the purchase of linen, clothing or fabrics or hire of same not including laundry services.

References – HMRC VAT Manual VATGPB10370 (24 March 2015)

http://www.hmrc.gov.uk/manuals/vatgpbmanual/VATGPB10370.htm

33 - *Library services*

This includes the provision of library services (such as the supply of information) by an external contractor or supplier e.g. a university or academic institution, including electronic or online library services or internet hosted library services and access to professional journals (including "subscriptions").

It excludes website subscriptions (but see above) and subscriptions to publications or online journals or publications (i.e. where there is a subscription to a specific publication but not a library service).

Notes – subscription may be a misnomer in this context. A subscription normally is an ineligible service but if the "subscription" is actually a charge for online library services or online access to journals then it is eligible for recovery under this Heading. Subscriptions to websites or to an individual publication are not eligible.

References – HMRC VAT Manual VATGPB10390 (24 March 2015)

http://www.hmrc.gov.uk/manuals/vatgpbmanual/VATGPB10390.htm

34 - Maintenance and care of livestock and fauna in connection with the Royal Parks

This includes the services related to the maintenance and care of livestock and fauna in connection with the Royal Parks such as:

- veterinary costs
- tree surgeons' services
- vaccination programmes

References – HMRC VAT Manual VATGPB10410 (24 March 2015)

http://www.hmrc.gov.uk/manuals/vatgpbmanual/VATGPB10410.htm

35 - Maintenance, non-structural repair and cleaning of buildings

This includes the maintenance, repair or cleaning of buildings by an external contractor or supplier funded from revenue expenditure. Maintenance or repair relates to existing buildings, structures or premises as opposed to new construction or new work. Also includes cleaning of any kind e.g. domestic services as well as steam cleaning or window cleaning and also redecoration. Also the maintenance of gardens and grounds including tree surgery, grass cutting, surface maintenance, road cleaning and gardening (but not landscaping). Also any materials used in the repair or maintenance work.

It excludes the maintenance, repair or cleaning of buildings by an external contractor or supplier funded from capital expenditure and new construction or new work as well as alterations, conversions, extensions, additions, or improvements. Also excludes initial decorating services and the separate purchase of cleaning materials. Also the supply or installation of goods, plant or equipment (plant means an immovable item which is genuinely fixed in the sense of being permanently incorporated into the structure of the building e.g. lifts, boilers and generators or other industrial equipment).

References – p51 *Guidance Notes for Government Departments* Seventh Edition Issued: 19 July 2012.

HMRC have produced the table below as a guide to recovery under Heading 35 and also Heading 37 where it relates to installed plant or equipment (but subject to the requirement that the works are funded from revenue expenditure).

CONTRACTED-OUT SERVICES

	Subject	Description	Recovery	COS Heading
1.	Alarms	Repairing existing fire/burglar alarms	Yes	35
		Installation of fire/burglar alarms	No	NA
		Extension to current systems	No	NA
		Repair by partial replacement of parts within existing fire/burglar alarm	Yes	35
		The complete replacement of an existing system	No	NA
2.	Asbestos	Removing asbestos	Yes	35
		Sealing in asbestos	Yes	35
3.	Ceilings	Repairing existing ceiling/suspended ceiling	Yes	35
		Replacing existing damaged tiles in same location (within existing grids structure)	Yes	35
		Forming fire breaks in ceiling voids	No	NA
		Construction of new ceiling/suspended ceilings.	No	NA
		Complete replacement of suspended ceiling structure	No	NA
4.	Construction	Building new cool room	No	NA
		Construction of a new room	No	NA
		Building new extension	No	NA
		Major building improvements	No	NA
		Installation of a new damp proof course	No	NA
		Installation of a silicone based injection.	No	NA
		Single supply of scaffolding	No	NA
		Structural repairs not traditionally performed in-house, as the work requires highly specialised skills.	No	NA
5.	Decorating	Painting and decorating existing walls, windows etc to restore decorative order	Yes	35
		First time decoration	No	NA
6.	Doors	Resealing against damp and draughts	Yes	35
		Fitting fire doors in corridors to form a fire break	No	NA
		Widening doors to allow wheelchair access	No	NA
		Blocking up old/existing doorways	No	NA

		Installing new doors/door frames where none existed previously	No	NA
		Installation of automatic/electric doors	No	NA
		First time fitting of fire doors in new buildings/ extensions	No	NA
		Fitting fire doors in new partitions	No	NA
7.	Electrical	Electrical works would include items such as installation of luminaries, general lighting, small power, nurse call systems, electrical connections to other systems. VAT recovery will be dependent upon the context of the specific job being undertaken, e.g. if purely refurbishment, more scope expected for VAT recovery. If major alteration/reconfiguration, limited scope for recovery.		
		Extension of wiring into new areas	No	NA
		Installation of new emergency lighting/fire signs	No	NA
		Installation/replacement of Building Management System	No	NA
		Installing new/additional wiring and/or sockets	No	NA
		Installing new/additional wiring and/or light fittings	No	NA
		Installing new/addition cables/wiring for telephone/data lines	No	NA
		Complete removal and replacement of wiring back to distribution boards	No	NA
8.	Fire Escapes	Repairing fire escapes	Yes	35
		Replacing fire escapes	No	NA
		Building new fire escapes	No	NA
9.	Flooring	Breaking up existing concrete floors and subsequent relaying at a slight different floor level.	Yes	35
		Repairing existing stuck down flooring by rescreeding and resurfacing bonded fitted flooring, including stuck down carpet, carpet tiles, floor tiles and vinyl.	Yes	35
		Supplying first time flooring	No	NA

		Installing plywood base to level floor	No	NA
		Replacing fitted carpets (i.e. not stuck down)	No	NA
10.	Grounds	Gardening	Yes	35
		Grass cutting	Yes	35
		Tree surgery	Yes	35
		Landscaping/redesigning grounds	No	NA
11.	Incinerators	Repair of incinerator	Yes	37
		Installing new incinerator	No	NA
		Construction/extending height of chimney	No	NA
		Replacement of incinerator	No	NA
12.	Insulation	Increasing thickness of existing lagging on incinerators	No	NA
		First time installing of insulation	No	NA
		Installing sound proofing panels	No	NA
13.	Kitchen	Repair by resurfacing existing worktops and units	Yes	35
		Installing/building new kitchen units, cupboards etc.	No	NA
		Installing/building new work tops.	No	NA
14.	Lift	Repair of lift	Yes	37
		Replacement of lift	No	NA
		Installing a new lift	No	NA
15.	Mechanical	Mechanical works would include items such as pipework, ductwork, heating units, chiller units, chilled water plant, air handling units, hot and cold water plant, compressed air systems, medical gases and soil and waste pipework.		
		Repairs to faulty systems (including parts)	Yes	37
		Replacement of system	No	NA
		Installation of new system	No	NA
		Alterations/additions and extensions to existing system	No	NA
		Fixing values and/or meters to existing/new radiators, pipes and taps to regulate temperate of hot water for patient safety/energy conservation purposes	Yes	37

		Repair existing pipes/radiators	Yes	37
		Installation of new/addition piles/radiators	No	NA
		Replacing water tanks	No	NA
		Building/installing new water tanks	No	NA
		First time installation of boiler	No	NA
		Replacement of boiler	No	NA
		Repair to boiler (including parts)	Yes	37
		Complete replacement of central heating system	No	NA
		Installation of new central heating system	No	NA
		Testing and Commissioning	No	NA
16.	Miscellaneous	Minor works of a repair and maintenance nature	Yes	35
		Disturbance works, where those works only need to be undertaken as a result of alterations to a building or as a result of new building works.	No	NA
		Fitting of fire hoses/extinguishers	No	NA
		Fitting of grilles, bars, locks, window film and security cameras	No	NA
		Installation of shelves	No	NA
		Replacement of shelves	No	NA
17.	Ramps	Repair existing ramps/handrails for access for the disabled	Yes	35
		Replacing/altering of ramps/handrails	No	NA
		Initial provision of ramps/handrails including replacement of stairs/steps by ramps	No	NA
18.	Roads	Breaking up and removal of covers to existing manholes and their reprovision in the same place at a higher level	Yes	35
		Resurfacing existing car parks	Yes	35
		Resurfacing existing footpaths	Yes	35
		Relaying down to foundation of existing footpaths	No	NA
		Road cleaning	Yes	35
		Building new car park/footpath where one did not previously exist.	No	NA

19.	Roofs	Maintenance of roofs including necessary access works	Yes	35
		Resurfacing/replacing/reslating existing roof	Yes	35
		Re-felting of flat roofs	Yes	35
		Altering existing pitch i.e. replacing flat roof by pitch	No	NA
		Roofing over previous open space	No	NA
		Installation of canopy	No	NA
20.	Sanitary ware	Repair of existing damaged wash basins and sanitary ware.	Yes	35
		Fitting new wash basins and sanitary ware.	No	NA
		Replacing existing systems in new locations or replacing bath by shower, toilet by wash basin etc	No	NA
		Replacement of sanitary back and side panels, vanity units, shower cubicles.	No	NA
21.	Signs	Repairs to existing signs	Yes	37
		Repair by replacement signs	No	NA
		New signs necessary only as a result of a Trust merger	Yes	37
22.	Walls	Repairing existing partitions	Yes	35
		Restoration of damaged plaster work/brick work	Yes	35
		Constructing new partitions/walls, altering partition layout	No	NA
		First time fitting of partitions in new buildings/extensions	No	NA
		Painting new walls/partitions	No	NA
		Repairing damaged tiles	Yes	35
		Tiling new areas	No	NA
		Repairs to wall-cladding	Yes	35
		Provision of wall-cladding/wall panels/wall protection rails	No	NA
		Replacement wall-cladding/wall panels/wall protection rails	No	NA
23.	Windows	Repairing existing window frames and glass with similar items	Yes	35

		Bricking up windows or forming new window/window frames.	No	NA
		Installation of fitted blinds, curtains and curtain tracks	No	NA
		Replacement of fitted blinds, curtains and curtain tracks	No	NA
		Installation of combination window/blind units	No	NA
		Repair to fitted blinds, curtains and curtain tracks	Yes	37
24	Woodwork	Repairs to dado /picture rail and skirting boards	Yes	35
		Replacement of dado /picture rail and skirting boards	No	NA

36 - *Maintenance and repair of civil engineering works*

This includes the maintenance and repair of civil engineering works by an external contractor or supplier. Civil engineering works include bridges, drains etc (but not roads).

It excludes the repair and maintenance of roads (which is covered by Heading 6), new civil engineering projects or work carried out under a s.278 agreement (see Heading 6) and winter road gritting and cleaning services.

References – HMRC VAT Manual VATGPB10450 (24 March 2015)

http://www.hmrc.gov.uk/manuals/vatgpbmanual/VATGPB10450.htm

37 - *Maintenance, repair and cleaning of equipment, plant, vehicles and vessels*

This includes the maintenance, repair or cleaning of equipment, plant, vehicles or vessels by an external contractor or supplier including the cost of parts or materials or exchange units where this is part of a single (or composite) supply of services (and incidental to the supply of the services).

It excludes materials, parts or other goods except where these are part of a single (or composite) supply of services and incidental to the supply of the services i.e. materials, parts or other goods purchased separately are ineligible for recovery. Also excludes the installation of equipment and the maintenance of telephone lines (see Heading 14).

Notes – where the purchase price of goods includes a manufacturer's warranty this would be a single (or composite) supply of goods and VAT incurred on the warranty is not eligible for recovery as COS (even if the warranty charge is separately invoiced). Where a separate maintenance agreement is entered into after the expiry of the manufacturer's warranty then this service would be eligible for recovery under this Heading.

This Heading was revised in 2007 retrospective to 1 April 2006 (see below):

Heading 37 'Maintenance, repair and cleaning of equipment, plant, vehicles and vessels;' Treasury have additionally confirmed that recovery of VAT under this Heading can be extended to equipment, plant, vehicles and vessels leased by a department from a separate supplier to the one providing the maintenance. Recovery on this basis can be made with effect from 1st April 2006. Previously recovery was restricted to equipment, plant, vehicles and vessels owned by a department. Treasury have agreed that the previous restriction did not take sufficient recognition of the fact that many departments gain benefit in leasing rather than purchasing this sort of item outright.

The leasing or hire of equipment, plant, vehicles and vessels is however a supply of goods and any VAT incurred in respect of this is NOT recoverable. The only exceptions to this are headings 25 'Hire of reprographic equipment including repair and maintenance' and 26 'Hire of vehicles, including repair and maintenance'. In both these cases the VAT is only recoverable on contracts for the supply of the equipment /vehicles together with full repair and maintenance services.

The leasing or hire of equipment, plant, vehicles and vessels is actually a supply of services rather than a supply of goods as stated above but it remains an ineligible service and therefore not recoverable as COS.

Also it is no longer a condition in relation to leased equipment etc that the maintenance services must be provided by a different supplier to the supplier of the leased equipment. This condition has been clarified to exclude only contracts where it is mandatory to use the same supplier. Where a GD has an option to use either the supplier of the leased equipment or a separate supplier to provide maintenance services then recovery is allowed if the GD opts to use the same supplier.

References – p52 *Guidance Notes for Government Departments* Seventh Edition Issued: 19 July 2012.

38 - *Maintenance and repair of statues, monuments and works of art*
This includes the maintenance and repair of statues, monuments and works of art by an external contractor or supplier such as cleaning, restoration, removal or relocation.

It excludes costs relating to the design and installation of new monuments.

References – HMRC VAT Manual VATGPB10490 (24 March 2015)

39 - Medical and social surveys
This includes the supply of a medical or social survey by an external contractor or supplier. Also includes the provision of information from general surveys previously carried out.

It excludes costs incurred directly by a GD in procuring the service for itself unless these are otherwise eligible for recovery under another Heading and MORI polls as these have always been undertaken by independent external bodies to conduct opinion polls.

This Heading is specifically designed to allow recovery on surveys which were previously carried out in-house by GDs and which are now outsourced to private sector providers (and where the results are to be used in relation the non-business activities of the GD). This type of survey is most typically conducted amongst other public bodies such as local authorities, police authorities, health authorities and charities etc and the information obtained is used to inform future planning and policies. Other types of survey may also be eligible for recovery but the key criteria is to demonstrate that they are medical or social in nature and would have previously been undertaken in-house by a GD.

References – HMRC VAT Manual VATGPB10510 (24 March 2015)

http://www.hmrc.gov.uk/manuals/vatgpbmanual/VATGPB10510.htm

40 - Messenger, portering and reception services
This includes the supply of messenger, portering or reception services by an external contractor or supplier such as the internal movement of documents, mail or equipment. Also includes reception or receptionist services or appointment or reminder services.

It excludes the hire of telephone lines or telephone or switchboard equipment. Also excludes the supply of agency staff.

References – HMRC VAT Manual VATGPB10530 (24 March 2015)

http://www.hmrc.gov.uk/manuals/vatgpbmanual/VATGPB10530.htm

41 - Nursing services
This includes the provision of nursing services or agency nursing staff by an external contractor or supplier. Nursing services includes the services of auxiliaries as well as qualified or registered nursing staff.

It excludes the supply of agency medical staff other than nurses e.g. locums and PAMs etc.

Notes – the supply of nursing staff by an agency is standard-rated but by HMRC concession (VAT Notice 710/2/83) it may be treated as exempt (not all agencies operate the concession). The agency commission is standard-rated and is recoverable.

References – p53 *Guidance Notes for Government Departments* Seventh Edition Issued: 19 July 2012.

42 - *Office removals*
This includes the provision of an office removal service or office relocation services by an external contractor or supplier. Also hire of crates as part of a removal service.

It excludes the hire of crates without a corresponding removal service.

References – HMRC VAT Manual VATGPB10570 (24 March 2015)

http://www.hmrc.gov.uk/manuals/vatgpbmanual/VATGPB10570.htm

43 - *Operation and maintenance of static test facilities, engineering and support services and test range industrial support and security/safety services including those acquired for the purposes of research and development*
This includes the operation and maintenance of static test facilities, engineering and support services and test range industrial support and security/safety services including those acquired for the purposes of research and development by an external contractor or supplier.

References – HMRC VAT Manual VATGPB10590 (24 March 2015)

http://www.hmrc.gov.uk/manuals/vatgpbmanual/VATGPB10590.htm

44 - *Operation and maintenance of stores depots.*
This includes the operation and maintenance of stores depots by an external contractor or supplier. Also includes the provision of a stock management service.

It excludes any supply of goods or stock.

References – p54 *Guidance Notes for Government Departments* Seventh Edition Issued: 19 July 2012.

45 - *Operation of hospitals, health care establishments and health care facilities and the provision of any related services*
This includes the operation of hospitals, healthcare establishments or healthcare facilities and the provision of any related services by an external contractor or supplier. For a PFI or LIFT project the level of services provided is irrelevant; unitary charges are recoverable under this Heading even on a bare lease or "hard PFI". For non-PFI or LIFT projects also includes as part of comprehensive package of services in connection with

the operation of a hospital or healthcare establishment by an external contractor or supplier: the provision of non-clinical services; the supply of ancillary equipment (together with the service of operating and maintaining that equipment); the supply of utilities etc. Also includes the provision of related eligible services in a separate contract associated with a PFI or LIFT project, and the hire of MRI Scanners, Hyperbaric Chambers, Mobile Theatres or similar equipment. Recoverable when supplied as part of a PFI contract or otherwise, provided the equipment is supplied in conjunction with a supply of "staff presence of labour and expertise" (hire of the equipment itself is not recoverable). Also Heading 45 includes the facilities elements of Energy Management Contracts or Boiler House Schemes where these are eligible services (but not heat, energy or hot water which are supplies of goods). There must be a separate supply of an energy management service which comprises eligible services, and contracts cannot be artificially split (see **Appendix 11 – Supply**).

It excludes non-PFI or LIFT projects where minimal services are provided. It also excludes the hire of equipment without a staff presence from the supplier, and the supply of energy or hot water.

Notes – This Heading covers the provision of both PFI or LIFT and non-PFI (or LIFT) hospitals and healthcare establishments and healthcare facilities and was revised and clarified by HMRC in 2005:

> For these arrangements you should be looking first to see if it is a PFI arrangement and for the non-PFIs establish if there are sufficient services to facilitate the operation of a hospital, healthcare establishment or healthcare facility. When assessing the level of services provided with the building, it is important to consider the actual use of that building and that the services provided are consistent with that usage.

> This heading is intended to cover supplies made by a contractor who designs, builds, finances and provides all the non-clinical services, leaving the NHS trust to employ and direct the clinical staff. Related services, as it applies to the operation of hospitals, is intended to cover any services other than the supply of medical care.

> PFI or LIFT arrangements: Services element irrelevant – can be "hard" PFI, similar to 'bare' lease – VAT recoverable under the COS heading 45 rules.

> Non-PFI or LIFT hospitals and healthcare establishments and healthcare facilities: Minimal or no services – no VAT recoverable under COS heading 45 – if the services are supplied separately from the lease and are separately contracted for then the service elements may themselves be recoverable if they fall under any of the COS headings.

> Non-PFI or LIFT hospitals and healthcare establishments and healthcare facilities: Full package of services necessary for the operation of that

hospital etc. – for example estate management, reception, porterage, cleaning, laundry, catering, security, equipment maintenance, technicians – VAT recoverable under COS heading 45.

Arrangements for MRI scanners and similar medical equipment that is supplied with staff presence of labour and expertise remains eligible to be recovered under heading 45.

References – p54 *Guidance Notes for Government Departments* Seventh Edition Issued: 19 July 2012/ VAT Recovery under Headings 45 and 53 of the Contracted-Out Services Directions (HMRC 2005).

46 - *Operation of prisons, detention centres and remand centres, including medical services*

This includes the operation of prisons, detention centres and remand centres, including medical services by an external contractor or supplier such as:

- the operation of a private prison
- the operation of a prison shop
- prisoner transport services
- the operation of prison hospitals

Excludes hostel accommodation.

References – HMRC VAT Manual VATGPB10650 (24 March 2015)

http://www.hmrc.gov.uk/manuals/vatgpbmanual/VATGPB10650.htm

47 - *Passenger transport services*

This includes the provision of passenger transport services by an external contractor or supplier e.g. any vehicle supplied with a driver etc taxis, buses, minibuses etc. Also includes chauffeur driven vehicles and night car services.

It excludes costs incurred directly by a GD in procuring the service for itself unless otherwise eligible for recovery under another Heading. It also excludes the hire of vehicles without drivers or non-contracted taxi fares. Also excludes insurance, road tax and public transport or ad hoc taxi hires by staff.

References – HMRC VAT Manual VATGPB10670 (24 March 2015)

http://www.hmrc.gov.uk/manuals/vatgpbmanual/VATGPB10670.htm

48 - *Pest control services*

This includes the provision of a pest control service by an external contractor or supplier, such as disinfestation services, setting of traps, spraying insecticide and the removal of dead rodents.

It excludes the purchase of pest control substances, poisons, traps or materials.

References – HMRC VAT Manual VATGPB10690 (24 March 2015)

http://www.hmrc.gov.uk/manuals/vatgpbmanual/VATGPB10690.htm

49 - Photographic, reprographic, graphic and design services

This includes the provision of photographic, reprographic and design services by an external contractor or supplier. Also includes the hire of a photographer, photography services including photographs, the design & printing of reports, promotion or educational material or other similar material. Also the initial design of a web site.

It excludes the ongoing design or upgrading of websites.

References – p55 *Guidance Notes for Government Departments* Seventh Edition Issued: 19 July 2012.

50 - Preparation and despatch of forms

This includes the preparation and despatch of forms by an external contractor or supplier such as the design, printing and mailing of forms providing these services are provided within a single contract.

References – HMRC VAT Manual VATGPB10730 (24 March 2015)

http://www.hmrc.gov.uk/manuals/vatgpbmanual/VATGPB10730.htm

51 - Press cutting services

This includes the provision of a physical or electronic press cutting service by an external contractor or supplier.

References – HMRC VAT Manual VATGPB10750 (24 March 2015)

http://www.hmrc.gov.uk/manuals/vatgpbmanual/VATGPB10750.htm

52 - Professional Advice or opinion on departmental efficiency or policy issues, legal advice or opinion and internal audit.

The wording of this heading has been changed with Treasury agreement from "Professional services, including those of any manager, adviser, expert, specialist or consultant". The change in wording is designed to clarify the scope of recovery under the heading. The new wording reflects the intention that Heading 52 is essentially concerned with the provision of advice or information rather than the performance of the service itself. The scope of this Heading is intended to be narrow and only allows COS recovery in respect of advice on how to carry out or improve departmental functions or activities.

Includes:
- internal audit reports
- legal opinion

- management consultancy

Excludes:
- the hire of a consultant to work as part of the department (a supply of staff)
- the service of actually putting something into effect, as opposed to merely advising on a matter. For example, this Heading does not include the services of a professional who is brought in to advise on AND then implement a new initiative
- staff secondments
- specialist staff hired to provide "holiday/ maternity cover" for key staff members
- the hire of accountants to carry out tax health checks

Notes – the revised wording only applies to GDs as a matter of policy. The original wording applies to the NHS and the Treasury (Contracting-out) Directions and still has the force of law.

References – p56 *Guidance Notes for Government Departments* Seventh Edition Issued: 19 July 2012.

53 - *Provision under a PFI agreement of accommodation, for office or other governmental use, together with management or other services in connection with that accommodation*

This includes serviced or managed PFI arrangements for offices, and other government buildings. PFI agreements must include a management or service package.

This Heading covers PFI arrangements under which GDs are supplied with fully serviced and managed accommodation by a single PFI provider. The most distinct element will be that risk is transferred from the GD to the PFI provider. Consequently, the heading does not include leases granted by commercial landlords, even where they are landlord repairing and insuring leases.

If the building is used to carry on ...

- standard-rated business activities the input tax can be reclaimed under the normal VAT rules.
- exempt business activities then input tax cannot be recovered
- GD non-business activities then:
  if a building is occupied under a normal commercial lease the type of lease will invariably include, the landlord's obligation to maintain the building (for example, heat, light, utilities, cleaning, repairs and maintenance, and insurance); and, among the tenants' obligations, a covenant to pay rents and service charges – not recoverable under Heading 53

if a building is occupied under a PFI arrangement – recoverable under Heading 53

If you are unsure about the terms under which you occupy the building, please contact your department's procurement section. They will be able to advise whether your department is occupying the building under a normal commercial lease or has entered in to a Treasury approved PFI arrangement.

Where there is mixed use then there must be an apportionment between the business and non-business use.

Excludes any accommodation not provided under a PFI agreement. Also excludes PFI accommodation where no services are provided or which is used to make exempt supplies.

Notes – this Heading covers the provision of serviced or managed accommodation under a PFI arrangement and was clarified by HMRC in 2005:

Heading 53: Covers PFI arrangements for offices, and other government buildings that are serviced or managed (excluding hospitals and health care establishments)

Situation

All non-PFI arrangements: Level of services provided irrelevant – no VAT recoverable under COS heading 53. If the services are supplied separately from the lease and are separately contracted for then the service elements may themselves be recoverable if they fall under any of the COS headings.

PFI arrangements with lease of serviced or managed office or other Public Sector accommodation (other than hospital and healthcare falling under heading 45) of any duration – VAT recoverable under COS heading 53.

PFI arrangements for the lease of accommodation only (i.e. no management and other services) – no VAT recoverable

Contract debtor PFI arrangements (that is, arrangements where there is no initial lease of the property to the service provider) should be treated in the same manner as traditional PFI arrangements and included in this category for VAT recovery purposes as long as all of the necessary conditions for VAT recovery are satisfied.

References – p57 *Guidance Notes for Government Departments* Seventh Edition Issued: 19 July 2012/VAT Recovery under Headings 45 and 53 of the Contracted-Out Services Directions (HMRC 2005).

54 - Publicity services

This includes the provision of publicity services by an external contractor or supplier e.g. a PR company, advertising or media agency.

It excludes the direct placement of advertisements or other costs incurred directly by a GD unless these are otherwise eligible for recovery under another Heading.

References – p58 *Guidance Notes for Government Departments* Seventh Edition Issued: 19 July 2012.

55 - Purchasing and procurement services

This includes the provision of purchasing or procurement services by an external contractor or supplier such as a buying or purchasing agent.

It excludes any supply of goods or equipment.

References – p58 *Guidance Notes for Government Departments* Seventh Edition Issued: 19 July 2012.

56 - Radio services

This includes the provision of radio services by an external contractor or supplier.

It excludes the supply of radio equipment or any other costs incurred directly unless these are otherwise eligible for recovery under another Heading.

References – p58 *Guidance Notes for Government Departments* Seventh Edition Issued: 19 July 2012.

57 - Recruitment and relocation of staff and other related services

This includes the provision of recruitment services and relocation of staff services and other related services by an external contractor or supplier such as a recruitment agency or consultancy or a relocation agency. Also includes security vetting checks undertaken on employees and staff recruitment advertising commissioned via a recruitment agency.

It excludes the direct placement of recruitment advertisements or other costs incurred directly unless these are otherwise eligible for recovery under another Heading and costs incurred directly by staff e.g. on removal firms.

References – p58 *Guidance Notes for Government Departments* Seventh Edition Issued: 19 July 2012.

58 - Research, testing, inspection, certification and approval work for the Health and Safety Executive

This includes research, testing, inspection, certification and approval work for the HSE by an external contractor or supplier.

Devolved administrations discharging functions on behalf of the HSE are eligible to recover COS under this Heading.

References – HMRC VAT Manual VATGPB10890 (24 March 2015)

http://www.hmrc.gov.uk/manuals/vatgpbmanual/VATGPB10890.htm

59 - Scientific work of the kind normally carried out for the Department of the Environment, Food and Rural Affairs and the Food Standards Agency

This includes scientific work of the kind normally carried out for the Department of the Environment, Food and Rural Affairs and the Food Standards Agency by an external contractor or supplier such as:

- testing contaminated food
- detection and verification of disease in animals
- detection and verification of plant disease
- inspection of diseased animal carcases

This Heading may be used by departments in the devolved administrations if they have taken over responsibility for work undertaken by DEFRA or the FSA.

References – HMRC VAT Manual VATGPB10910 (24 March 2015)

http://www.hmrc.gov.uk/manuals/vatgpbmanual/VATGPB10910.htm

60 - Security services

This includes the provision of security services by an external contractor or supplier such as the provision of security guards, patrols and secure transport etc and security equipment where it is an intrinsic element of the service e.g. surveillance cameras or CCTV.

It excludes the direct procurement of security equipment or other costs incurred directly unless these are otherwise eligible for recovery under another Heading. Also excludes the hire of security staff to supplement in-house security teams and security vetting.

References – HMRC VAT Manual VATGPB10930 (24 March 2015)

http://www.hmrc.gov.uk/manuals/vatgpbmanual/VATGPB10930.htm

61 - Services of printing, copying, reproducing or mailing of any documents or publications, including typesetting services

This includes the services of printing, copying, reproducing or mailing any documents or publications including typesetting services by an external contractor or supplier. Also includes the printing or reproduction of reports, publications, letterheads, forms, labels etc and reprints where supplied to a specification; photocopying and mailing services; filing, filming and microfiche storage and retrieval; and the printing of signs for an organisational merger and the repair of existing signs. Also includes post opening, franking, labelling and parcel x-raying services.

It excludes the supply of paper, inks or other goods related to printing where these are supplied separately. Also excludes the engraving of name badges or printing on t-shirts, pens or other items etc. and the printing of new signs not for the purposes of an organisational merger. Also excludes the hire of post boxes, franking and shredding machines.

References – p59 *Guidance Notes for Government Departments* Seventh Edition Issued: 19 July 2012.

62 - Share registry survey

This includes the provision of share registry survey services by an external contractor or supplier.

References – HMRC VAT Manual VATGPB10970 (24 March 2015)

http://www.hmrc.gov.uk/manuals/vatgpbmanual/VATGPB10970.htm

63 - Storage, distribution and goods disposal services

This includes the provision of physical or electronic storage, distribution or goods disposal services by an external contractor or supplier, such as the archiving of documents or record storage and retrieval services. Also includes the storage of goods, equipment or stock etc or the distribution of goods, equipment or stock etc. and the destruction of documents or the disposal of goods, equipment or stock or incineration services. Also includes the storage of detained or seized items and their secure disposal, the accommodation of seized or detained animals in zoos or boarding kennels etc, the storage of employees' possessions when they are relocated, secure bulk shredding services and call-off stock.

Notes – Changes were introduced by the Finance Act 2012 which required the standard rate of VAT to be applied to supplies of storage facilities with effect from 1 October 2012 (VATLP17550).

http://www.hmrc.gov.uk/manuals/vatlpmanual/VATLP17550.htm
http://www.hmrc.gov.uk/manuals/vatlpmanual/VATLP17600.htm

References – HMRC VAT Manual VATGPB10990 (24 March 2015)

http://www.hmrc.gov.uk/manuals/vatgpbmanual/VATGPB10990.htm

64 - Surveying, certification and registration in connection with ships and relevant record-keeping and verification, issue of certification, cards, discharge books and campaign medals to seamen

This includes the services of surveying, certification and registration in connection with ships and relevant record-keeping and verification, issue of certification cards, discharge books and campaign medals to seamen by an external contractor or supplier.

References – HMRC VAT Manual VATGPB11010 (24 March 2015)

http://www.hmrc.gov.uk/manuals/vatgpbmanual/VATGPB11010.htm

65 - *Training, tuition or education*

This includes the provision of training, tuition or education by an external contractor or supplier such as the services of trainers or lecturers. Also includes packages which include room hire for training or accommodation for students. Also includes online training.

It excludes room hire for training or accommodation for students when supplied separately and training materials such as DVDs and stationery when supplied separately.

Notes – training provided by an eligible body is an exempt supply and therefore no VAT will be charged (VAT Notice 701/30). Eligible bodies include NHS and GDs, Universities, Further Education Colleges and other educational institutions, professional bodies and charities. In practice, VAT will only be charged on training by private sector businesses. Self-employed trainers or lecturers may not be registered for VAT.

References – HMRC VAT Manual VATGPB11030 (24 March 2015)

http://www.hmrc.gov.uk/manuals/vatgpbmanual/VATGPB11030.htm

66 - *Transport research of the kind normally carried out for the Department for Transport*

This includes the provision of transport research services of the kind normally carried out for the Department of Transport by an external contractor or supplier.

Departments in the devolved administrations which carry out functions delegated to them by the Department of Transport may recover VAT incurred on transport research under this Heading.

References – HMRC VAT Manual VATGPB11050 (24 March 2015)

http://www.hmrc.gov.uk/manuals/vatgpbmanual/VATGPB11050.htm

67 - *Travel services, excluding hotel accommodation and fares*

This includes the provision of travel services by an external contractor or supplier such as the making of travel arrangements by a travel agent or external booking agency and charges for the use of VIP lounges at airports or stations.

It excludes hotel accommodation and fares (public transport services are generally zero-rated). Also excludes third party hired cars and taxi fares.

References – HMRC VAT Manual VATGPB11070 (24 March 2015)

http://www.hmrc.gov.uk/manuals/vatgpbmanual/VATGPB11070.htm

68 - *Travel and transport surveys, including traffic census counts*

This includes travel and transport surveys, including traffic census counts, carried out by an external contractor or supplier.

References – HMRC VAT Manual VATGPB11090 (24 March 2015)

http://www.hmrc.gov.uk/manuals/vatgpbmanual/VATGPB11090.htm

69 - *Typing secretarial, telephonist and clerical services including agency staff*

This includes supplies by agencies providing typing, secretarial, telephonist and clerical services using their own staff (but not a supply of staff by a recruitment agency) e.g. the provision of typing services by a word processing bureau.

It excludes direct supplies of agency staff, secondees and employee expenses.

References – p61 *Guidance Notes for Government Departments* Seventh Edition Issued: 19 July 2012.

70 - *Waste disposal services*

This includes the collection and disposal of waste, including the removal or disposal of ash, refuse and sludge by an external contractor or supplier. Also includes clinical waste disposal, incineration services, the hire of incineration facilities and the removal, conveyance, treatment or disposal of the contents of cesspools, septic tanks or similar, and the hire of rubbish bins, wheelie bins, skips or other receptacles where they are exchanged for empty ones by an external contractor or supplier. Also includes refuse collection, trade waste, feminine hygiene services and recycling services.

It excludes the purchase of waste disposal equipment or the hire without exchange or uplift of rubbish bins, wheelie bins or other receptacles, and the removal of waste from a building side post-demolition.

Notes – the disposal of construction or building waste is covered by Heading 35 (but excludes post-demolition waste which is not recoverable).

References – HMRC VAT Manual VATGPB11130 (24 March 2015)

http://www.hmrc.gov.uk/manuals/vatgpbmanual/VATGPB11130.htm

71 - *Welfare services*

This includes the provision of care, treatment or instruction designed to promote the physical or mental well-being of elderly, distressed or disabled persons, including children and young persons by an external contractor or supplier. Also includes staff support and counselling services.

Notes – welfare services are generally exempt supplies and therefore no VAT should be charged by the supplier.

References – HMRC VAT Manual VATGPB11150 (24 March 2015)

http://www.hmrc.gov.uk/manuals/vatgpbmanual/VATGPB11150.htm

72 - Career guidance, mentoring, counselling and other related services to help people in to work or to retain work as part of the DWP/Jobcentre Plus Employment Programme, provided under sections 2 and 9 of the Employment and Training Act 1973

This includes career guidance, mentoring, counselling and other related services to help people in to work or to retain work as part of the DWP/Jobcentre Plus Employment Programme, provided under sections 2 and 9 of the Employment and Training Act 1973 by an external contractor or supplier.

Notes – although this Heading refers to the DWP etc it is to be read as including any equivalent programme in Scotland, Wales or Northern Ireland.

References – HMRC VAT Manual VATGPB11170 (24 March 2015)

http://www.hmrc.gov.uk/manuals/vatgpbmanual/VATGPB11170.htm

73 - Services relating to Action Teams for Jobs and Employment Zones

The previous Heading which allowed recovery on "mentoring and counselling to help people in to work as part of the New Deal and ONE Programme" has been withdrawn. This is because activities which used to fall under this heading have largely been absorbed into the reworded Heading 72.

References – HMRC VAT Manual VATGPB11190 (24 March 2015)

http://www.hmrc.gov.uk/manuals/vatgpbmanual/VATGPB11190.htm

74 - Original research undertaken in order to gain knowledge and understanding

This includes research undertaken by an external contractor or supplier.

It excludes the direct cost of goods incurred by a GD and the direct cost of services incurred by a GD in relation to research unless eligible under another COS Heading.

Notes – research may be taxable or a non-business activity depending on the status or location of the supplier and the status or location of the recipient therefore a VAT charge may not be received on research services. The exemption on research supplied between eligible bodies was withdrawn on 1 August 2013 as contrary to EU law. Research services provided by private sector organisations will generally be standard-rated and where granted funded (including under a collaborative arrangement) research will generally be non-business.

HMRC interprets the term 'original research' as meaning research that:

- involves surveys, field tests or new research design thinking, interviews or observation conducted specifically in relation to the subject of the research (as opposed to merely collating existing data); and
- extends to secondary data analysis, interpretation (which may include options and/or recommendations) or a systemic review of evidence (rather than mere data gathering and recording)

References – HMRC VAT Manual VATGPB11210 (24 March 2015)

http://www.hmrc.gov.uk/manuals/vatgpbmanual/VATGPB11210.htm

75 - *Inspection of woodland sites for approval of felling licence applications and of timber imports/imports using timber packing to prevent entry of foreign tree pests and diseases*

This includes the inspection of woodland sites for approval of felling licence applications and of timber imports/imports using timber packing to prevent entry of foreign tree pests and diseases by an external contractor or supplier.

References – HMRC VAT Manual VATGPB11230 (24 March 2015)

http://www.hmrc.gov.uk/manuals/vatgpbmanual/VATGPB11230.htm

76 - *Probation Services delivered under the Criminal Justice and Court Services Act 2000*

Recovery under this Heading is allowed as a matter of policy. It is not in the Treasury (Contracting-Out) Directions and has not been published in the London, Edinburgh or Belfast Gazettes.

This includes probation services now delivered under the Offender Management Act 2007 by an external contractor or supplier (rather than the Criminal Justice and Court Services Act 2000).

References – HMRC VAT Manual VATGPB11250 (24 March 2015)

http://www.hmrc.gov.uk/manuals/vatgpbmanual/VATGPB11250.htm

3.2.1 Additional recovery

In addition the following services have been agreed by the Treasury for inclusion in the next revision of the directions and therefore COS may now be recovered in relation to these.

(i) call centre and contact centre services:
- VAT incurred by consumer direct call centres recoverable from 1 April 2007 (no entitlement to recover prior to this date)
- all other call centres recoverable from 1 April 2011 (no entitlement to recover prior to this date)

This includes:
- when a GD contracts out the management and day to day operation of contact Centres and Call Centres to third parties, and
- on the associated costs which are recharged by their suppliers
- and on the outsourced operation of the NHS 111 service

It excludes overheads relating to the provisions of in-house call centres and contact centres.

(ii) services provided through International Trade Advisers for UK Trade and Investment.

Recovery from 1 April 2011 (no entitlement to recover prior to this date).

(iii) services provided under Framework for Procuring External Support for Commissioners (FESC) other than:

- supplies of computer services and professional services that are excluded from the scope of Headings 14 and 52 above (unless Treasury directs otherwise).
- elsewhere, the supply of staff.

Recovery from 1 April 2007 (no entitlement to recover prior to this date).

4   Business Activities

4.1   Business Activities

Any income or transaction which falls within the scope of VAT Act 1994 s.4 is a business or economic activity (including by virtue of s.95 any trade profession or vocation and the provision by a club, association or organisation, for a subscription or other consideration, of the facilities or advantages available to its members, and the admission, for a consideration, of persons to any premises). There have been several cases in which the meaning of business in a VAT context has been examined.

Until 2012 any income, transaction or activity listed in the Treasury (Taxing) Directions revised in October 2008 was deemed to be a business activity for GDs (see **Appendix 5**) but VAT Act 1994 s.41 was amended in the Finance Act 2012 to clarify the position under EU law (see **Appendix 1**) and the Treasury (Taxing) Directions were repealed in relation to external bodies (although it still applies to supplies between GDs). HMRC have indicated that there should be no material change in the application of s.41; merely that in its revised form it is more consistent with the Principal VAT Directive in relation to distortion of competition.

The main business activities of GDs include:
- sales of goods
- supplies of services
- supplies of land and property

4.1.1   Output tax

If the income, transaction or activity does fall within the scope of the tax then output tax will be chargeable unless it falls within Schedule 8 (Zero-Rate) or Schedule 9 (Exempt) of the VAT Act 1994. All supplies of goods or services within the scope of the tax are standard-rated (20%) unless specifically excluded (if a supply falls within Schedule 7A (Reduced-Rate) then output tax will be chargeable at 5% rather than 20%). Theoretically, output tax charged is payable by the final consumer and therefore has no net effect on the position of the supplier making a taxable supply.

When a GD makes supplies of goods or services to another GD this is a supply for VAT purposes and VAT must be charged at the appropriate rate. However, if a sale is made between parts of a GD i.e. within the same taxable person, or between a GD and its executive agency registered under the same VAT registration number, this is not a supply for VAT purposes and is disregarded. If a GD makes taxable supplies to an NDPB the normal rules apply. An Executive Agency which is not separately registered will not charge VAT on any supplies it makes to its parent GD, as the supply is within the same taxable person and is therefore disregarded. An Executive Agency or Trading Fund which has been separately registered for VAT must charge VAT on their standard-rated and reduced-rate supplies including supplies to their parent GDs.

4.1.2   Input tax

VAT incurred by a taxable person which is attributable to business activities will be input tax, but not necessarily allowable input tax.

For input tax to qualify as allowable under s.26 of the Act it must be:
- attributable to a taxable supply;
- attributable to supplies outside the UK which would be taxable supplies if made within the UK; and
- attributable to an exempt supply (but within the de minimis limits).

The entitlement to deduct arises in relation to goods acquired or services received for the purpose of business. This means that the taxable supply to which the input tax is attributable need not have actually occurred or be about to occur at the time the goods are acquired or services received. The intention to make a taxable supply also gives rise to the right to deduct. In certain circumstances that right also subsists where there is no subsequent taxable supply, but there are clawback and payback provisions under the VAT Regulations 1995 SI 1995/2518 where an intended taxable supply crystallises as an actual exempt supply or there is a change of use from taxable to exempt or vice versa (see *VAT Notice 706/1/11 Partial Exemption, para 13*).

There are three levels of input tax recovery:
- direct recovery on directly attributable input tax (full recovery in relation to wholly taxable supplies);
- indirect recovery on sectorised costs (where parts of the business can be separately analysed and a taxable % calculated); and
- residual recovery on general overheads (non-attributable input tax subject to a general and final apportionment).

Business/non-business apportionment

Input tax is either directly attributable or indirectly attributable. Direct attribution means wholly and exclusively attributable to a supply whether taxable or exempt (or a supply above) and where taxable it should be claimed in full in the VAT Return for period in which it is incurred. Direct input tax is not dependent on any method or special method and may be claimed without any further calculation or the approval of HMRC (subject to VAT Act 1994 s.26). Indirect attribution means partly attributable (to any degree) to taxable supplies (or a supply above) and partly attributable to exempt supplies or non-business activities or both. Indirect input tax may either be apportioned according a specific activity (sectorisation or partial attribution) or as part of all general and overhead costs (residual attribution). Sectorisation can be a very accurate apportionment depending on the information available but it remains indirect attribution. Residual attribution identifies the final residual input tax entitlement where no specific apportionment is feasible on general costs and overheads. The more intensive the analysis, the more detailed the method, the more accurate the attribution. However, while GDs are allowed as a matter of Treasury policy to apportion VAT incurred between business (input tax) and non-business activities (non-input tax) they are not allowed to carry out partial exemption calculations (but see **1.2.2 Trading Funds**).

Any business/non-business apportionment must result in a fair and reasonable attribution of input tax. The method the taxpayer uses to calculate the allowable input tax does not require the approval of HMRC because there is no provision in law which requires that HMRC approve a business/non-business apportionment method of itself. However, in practice, HMRC approve the method indirectly by approving the resulting input tax claimed as a fair and reasonable attribution.

Partial exemption

As a matter of Treasury policy GDs and Executive Agencies are not allowed to carry out partial exemption calculations but Trading Funds (which are generally wholly business entities) are allowed to do so subject to the Treasury approval and in conjunction with the Government Departments Team.

Partial exemption is an apportionment of input tax between taxable supplies and exempt supplies (subject to the *VAT Regulations 1995 SI 1995/2518 Part XIV – Input Tax and Partial Exemption*). A business which makes exempt supplies cannot reclaim all of its input tax and must use an approved partial exemption method which will normally be either the standard method (which does not require the prior written approval of HMRC) or a special method (which does require the prior written approval of HMRC).

The following are generally excluded from the calculation:
- supplies of capital goods or assets used for the purposes of the business whether or not subject to the Capital Goods Scheme;
- incidental financial transactions or income e.g. bank interest received;
- incidental land and property transactions e.g. a one-off sale of land (but generally not an ongoing supply of accommodation etc);

- any self-supply made e.g. a reverse charge supply (see **Chapter 6 International VAT**); and
- any transaction on which output tax is not chargeable by Treasury Order (*VAT Act 1994 s.25*) or any transactions which are not supplies for VAT purposes (as deemed by Treasury) e.g. the transfer of a business or part of a business as a going concern (TOGC).

Partial exemption calculations should be completed monthly (or quarterly if appropriate) on a provisional basis with an annual adjustment in Month 13 (the April VAT Return due by 31 May) for the "longer period" i.e. the financial year (this requirement does not apply to the business/non-business apportionment calculations). Where Returns are quarterly the annual adjustment can be done in the fourth quarter or the period immediately thereafter. Technically, the business/non-business apportionment calculation and the partial exemption calculation are separate, with the business/non-business apportionment being carried out first and the partial exemption calculation then applied to the business proportion. In 2011 a combined method was introduced which allows a business to carry out these calculations in combination. The combined method requires the prior written approval of HMRC and the partial exemption de minimis rule is disapplied (exempt input tax of less than £7,500 p.a. and not more than 50% of the total input tax can be claimed as fully taxable).

The objective of these calculations is to identify the proportion of allowable input tax a business is entitled to reclaim over the financial year (output tax is not affected or apportioned) and the overriding principle is that any method must give a fair and reasonable result. VAT is allowable input tax if consumed in the making of taxable supplies or otherwise allowable under VAT Act 1994 s.26. This cannot normally be ascertained directly from the data available (and the calculation is ultimately limited by the quality of the data available). Therefore, a proxy is used to calculate it indirectly e.g. income or outputs, but also potentially floorspace or transaction ratios, staff time ratios or purchases and inputs.

(see *VAT Notice 706 Partial Exemption*)

4.2 The Treasury List

Until the repeal of VAT Act 1994 s.41(2) in Finance Act 2012 the activities listed below listed below were deemed to be business activities by a GD by Treasury Direction (revised October 2008). The Treasury List now only has effect between GDs and does not apply in relation to any other business supplies.

Any activities:

- which may not amount to the carrying on of a business but where there may be competition with the private sector (other taxable persons carrying on a business);
- whether goods or services; and
- where supplied for a consideration (i.e. where a charge is made)

were deemed to be business activities (it may have been, for whatever reason, that the activity did not fall within the scope of tax but by virtue of the Treasury Direction was deemed to be a business activity). The Treasury Direction did not apply where there was a statutory duty, or where there was no consideration (these remained non-business). Equally, the Treasury Direction had no effect where an activity was an economic activity under the Principal VAT Directive or fell under VAT Act 1994 s.4. In those circumstances, it would have been of itself a business activity; the Treasury Direction only removed the uncertainty where an activity may have been construed as a non-business activity.

HMRC take the view that the repeal of s.41(2) will not result in any material change in the treatment of business activities by GDs and the liability notes set out below assume supplies made within the United Kingdom and for a consideration. Although the most recent Treasury (Contracting-Out) Directions were issued in December 2002 deemed business activities were revised in October 2008.

All business supplies within the UK are taxable and standard-rated unless specifically excluded (see **Appendix 7 Reduced-Rate Supplies**, **Appendix 8 Zero-Rated Supplies** and **Appendix 9 Exempt Supplies**).

All supplies below are assumed to be made for a consideration and within the UK unless otherwise stated.

Accommodation, including property acquisition and disposal and any related services
Supplies of commercial accommodation are exempt unless an option to tax is exercised in which case standard-rated (only allowed for GDs on disposals of land or property and then only with Treasury permission):

- the leasing or letting of land or property including government offices (exempt)
- acquisition or purchase of land or property including government buildings (exempt or standard-rated where an option to tax is exercised by the vendor)
- disposal or sales of land or property including government buildings (exempt or standard-rated where an option to tax is exercised (with Treasury permission)

- professional services related to land or property e.g. legal, architects, surveyors etc (standard-rated)

Sales of new (up to three years old) commercial buildings are standard-rated irrespective of an option to tax (see **Chapter 5 Land & Property**).

Administration services

Supplies of administrative services are standard-rated, including administration services related to financial services or the management of funds (including funds in trust) unless the services provided qualify for exemption as a financial service:

- general administration services (standard-rated)
- management, office, accounting or payroll services (standard-rated)
- administration services for shared services organisations (standard-rated)
- administration services for trading subsidiaries (standard-rated)
- administration of funds in trust (standard-rated)
- financial services administration (standard-rated)

(see *VAT Notice 701/49 Financial Services*)

Admission to premises and to events, e.g. entertainments, air displays etc
Supplies of admissions to premises and events are standard-rated including any kind of admission charge, concerts, open days, guided tours and firework displays.

However, the cultural exemption may apply to public or non-profit making bodies (eligible bodies) in certain circumstances and therefore the admission charges would be exempt (although not mandatory). Public bodies in this context include GDs, NDPBs listed in the Cabinet Office publication *'Public Bodies'* and local authorities. However, exemption cannot apply where the exemption of admission charges would be likely to distort competition to the disadvantage of a commercial supplier of similar services, or the public body enters into a joint venture or profit/income-making arrangement with anyone other than another public or eligible body.

An example of a joint venture which would not qualify for exemption is one where the local authority acts as a ticket broker for a commercial promoter or has a profit/income sharing arrangement with that promoter for a qualifying performance. An example of a joint venture which would qualify for exemption is one where the local authority sells tickets for a qualifying performance on behalf of an eligible body.

HMRC takes the view that it is entitled (under the terms of current EC agreements) to take a national and overall view of competition where admissions to the various cultural activities are supplied by public bodies. It is necessary therefore to establish at the outset whether commercial suppliers of cultural activities may be placed at relative disadvantage if similar supplies made by a particular public body are treated as exempt. However, once this has been done it is not necessary to apply this test to each future separate performance.

To satisfy the non-distortion requirement in order to exempt admissions of a qualifying nature a public body must take steps to notify all identifiable commercial suppliers of related facilities or performances. For example, a local authority will need to identify from its business rating, planning, taxation and other records, any such supplier within its geographical area of responsibility and to notify in writing its intention of introducing exemption to all those suppliers. This could be by individual letter or by public notice in the local press for the authority's geographical area, which will need to specify a date (for example, 30 days) by which any objection to exemption has to be lodged. The public body can start to exempt the supplies advertised for exemption but must retain copies of the relevant correspondence and advertisements for future examination.

Where there is an objection and the public body still wishes to exempt admission charges and disagrees with the objection, the public body should forward details of the intended exemption together with copies of the relevant correspondence to HMRC but it should not exempt any supplies which are in dispute until the matter has been resolved. In identifying commercial suppliers who may be disadvantaged by exemption, a public body will only need to look at museums, galleries, art exhibitions and zoos or theatrical, musical and choreographic performances in isolation. For example, a public body wishing to exempt admission charges to a museum would have to demonstrate that it would not disadvantage commercial museums, galleries, art exhibitions and zoos within its geographical area, but would not have to take account of commercial theatrical, musical and choreographical performances.

Correspondingly, in judging whether exemption of theatrical performances of a cultural nature would disadvantage a commercial supplier, it will be sufficient for the public body to take account of all commercial suppliers of theatrical, musical or choreographic performances within its geographical area – it will not be necessary to take account of commercial museums, galleries, art exhibitions or zoos.

(see *VAT Notice 701/47 Culture*)

BUSINESS ACTIVITIES

Advertising or publicity services
The liability of supplies of advertising or publicity services are as follows:
- advertising services (other than to charities) (standard-rated)
- sponsorship (but not donations) (standard-rated)
- donations (outside the scope of VAT)
- distribution of advertising material (standard-rated)
- rights over land for advertising space (a licence to occupy) e.g. hoardings, boards, display stands etc (exempt)
- rights over land for advertising space (a licence to occupy) e.g. hoardings, boards, display stands etc (standard-rated where an option to tax has been exercised)
- advertising services supplied to charities (zero-rated)

Archives
Supplies of archiving services are standard-rated including the archiving, maintaining and updating of records.

Attendance of staff at court (or any similar place)
Supplies of staff attendance at court are standard-rated including expert witness services and medico-legal services (standard-rated).

Bankruptcies and insolvency services
Supplies of professional services in relation to bankruptcy or insolvency are standard-rated.

Broadcasting services
Supplies of broadcasting services are standard-rated.

Car leasing
Supplies of car leasing services are standard-rated.

Catering, including supplies from vending machines
Supplies of catering are standard-rated or zero-rated depending on the type of activity.

Catering means the supply of prepared food and drink consumed on the premises where supplied involving a significant element of service (*VAT Notice 709/1*). It includes supplies made in restaurants, cafes and canteens (excluding cold takeaway food) and food prepared and supplied for events and functions. It does not include the retail supply of food such as pre-packed sandwiches or groceries which are zero-rated supplies of goods, nor does it include the retail supply of confectionery, crisps, ice cream or alcoholic drinks which are standard-rated supplies of goods.

The main aspects of catering by as a business activity by GDs are:

- catering on premises in staff and visitor restaurants, cafés or canteens etc (standard-rated)
- catering at events and functions (standard-rated)
- vending machine sales in staff and visitor restaurants, cafés or canteens etc (standard-rated – or partly zero-rated subject to a Retail Scheme apportionment – see *VAT Notice 727 Retail Schemes*)
- cold takeaway food sold in staff and visitor restaurants, cafés or canteens etc (zero-rated subject to a Retail Scheme apportionment – see *VAT Notice 727 Retail Schemes*)

Retail supplies as a business activity by GDs include:
- vending machine sales outside catering premises in common areas or thoroughfares (standard-rated or zero-rated depending on the product)
- sales of food and groceries etc (predominantly zero-rated)
- sales of confectionery, crisps and ice cream etc (standard-rated)

(retail supplies may be made from the catering outlets as well as shops etc – see **Appendix 7 Reduced-Rate Supplies** and **Appendix 8 Zero-Rated Supplies**).

The following tests determine whether or not an activity is "catering" and therefore the liability of the supplies made (these may be standard-rated or zero-rated):
- does it fall within the ordinary meaning of catering?
- is it supplied for consumption on the premises?
- is it hot food?

The ordinary meaning of "catering" is the definition above. Following *Compass Contract Services UK Ltd* (CA 2006) the definition of "premises" was revised and limited to areas controlled by the supplier or areas specifically provided for the consumption of food e.g. a seating area adjacent to a catering outlet (historically, the definition was much wider). The significance of the redefinition is that if cold food is taken away from these areas e.g. from a canteen back to an office in the same building then that will qualify for zero-rating. Hot takeaway, however, is standard-rated and "hot" means heated for consumption above the ambient temperature (including where a microwave is provided for customers to heat the food themselves – it does not, however, include items cooked and allowed to cool). The main area of uncertainty is over the supply of cold food which is prepared and delivered e.g. sandwich platters or cold buffets. Casual or ad hoc sales of sandwiches or cold savouries in offices etc are regarded as zero-rated retail supplies but contracted or commissioned sales (for meetings etc) are regarded as standard-rated catering supplies.

BUSINESS ACTIVITIES

Output tax

Output tax is due on the standard-rated sales and there are two methods of calculating the proportions of standard-rated and zero-rated sales. Whichever basis is chosen the VAT fraction is then applied to the standard-rated proportion of sales to calculate the output tax due. The balance is zero-rated and no output tax is due on this.

The first method is the Point of Sale Retail Scheme (*VAT Notice 727 Retail Schemes*). This is potentially the most accurate method of accounting for VAT on mixed liability sales. It involves the use of separate tills or a till system capable of distinguishing between goods sold at different rates of VAT. It is, however, subject to human error and depends on the staff operating the tills to always ask whether the supply is "sit-in" or "takeaway" and always to record the liability of the supply correctly.

The second (and more common) method is to use the Catering Adaptation Retail Scheme (CARS)(*VAT Notice 727 Retail Schemes*). With the permission of HMRC this can be used where sales do not exceed £1m annually (from any single site – different sites could potentially use different Retail Schemes depending on circumstances), the result is fair and reasonable and HMRC are satisfied that it is impracticable to operate the Point of Sale Scheme. The CARS operates in four steps:

(1) add up daily gross takings (including cash received, vouchers etc);
(2) calculate the percentage of total supplies of catering which is standard-rated – this is done by keeping a representative sample of standard-rated and zero-rated sales – this means catering staff keeping a manual record of the types of supply made for a period (and every site would require its own representative sample taken) – normally a seven day sample is satisfactory for HMRC and this should be updated annually – it should also take account of seasonal variations and fluctuations etc (if applicable);
(3) apply the percentage of standard-rated sales derived from the sample to the daily gross takings; and finally
(4) apply the VAT fraction to the standard-rated sales to calculate the output tax due.

There is a potential anomaly in relation to vending machines which has to be taken into account. Where these are sited outside catering premises e.g. in common areas or thoroughfares, sales are treated as retail supplies of goods and the liability is that of the product supplied. Where sited in staff and visitor restaurants, cafés or canteens etc the supply is regarded as standard-rated catering but subject to apportionment under the Retail Scheme used. Where this is the Catering Adaptation the representative sample taken should include any vending machine sales but if Point of Sale a separate and additional calculation will have to be carried out for the vending machine sales or all of the income may be incorrectly treated as standard-rated when it is partly zero-rated.

Input tax

Input tax is allowable on the direct and indirect costs attributable to taxable supplies of catering and food.

For GDs there are two levels of input tax recovery related to catering and food:

- Full recovery on directly attributable input tax – such as the cost of retail purchases where these are standard-rated (e.g. confectionery etc) or costs attributable to a catering outlet which is fully taxable such as a restaurant, café or bistro which caters only to staff or visitors – the zero-rated cold takeaway food does not normally give rise to a direct input tax entitlement because it is unlikely that VAT will have been charged on the purchases but zero-rated supplies are taxable supplies and there would be full Input tax entitlement on attributable costs if the catering outlet is fully taxable.

- Proportionate recovery on sectorised costs such as the catering cost centres – where costs can be wholly and exclusively attributed to a fully taxable outlet then they would fall into the category above but this is not normally the case except for peripheral and self-contained outlets such as coffee shops etc – this percentage is then applied to the sectorised costs and that proportion of the VAT incurred is allowable input tax – GDs are not allowed to be partly exempt and therefore any apportionment would be between taxable business supplies and non-business activities.

Proportionate recovery on capital expenditure will also be allowable – significant sums of VAT may be incurred in relation to capital expenditure and this area of entitlement is often overlooked – the entitlement arises in relation to taxable supplies made or intended to be made irrespective of whether the project is refurbishment, new build, alteration, extension etc – the amount of input tax allowable will depend on the proportion of the VAT incurred which relates or will relate to taxable supplies – further calculations will be necessary to determine this proportion – but typically it would be based on a floorspace analysis and ratio based on the split between taxable business supplies and non-business activities – from 1 January 2011 any capital project with a net value in excess of £250,000 and including a business element (taxable or exempt) falls within the Capital Goods Scheme (see **5.6 Capital Goods Scheme**).

BUSINESS ACTIVITIES

Community Tradeable Emissions Allowances (in return for payment pursuant to section 16 of the Finance Act 2007 where such allowances could also be obtained from the Private Sector)

Supplies of community tradeable emissions allowances are zero-rated.

(*The Value Added Tax (Emissions Allowances) Order 2009*)

Computer services or goods
Supplies of computer services or goods are standard-rated.

Concessions for catering or other services
Supplies of concessions for catering or other related services are standard-rated where there is a concession with profit share e.g. retail outlets or where there is a concession as a right over land (where an option to tax has been exercised) e.g. retail outlets (a licence to occupy).

Supplies of concessions for catering or other related services are exempt where there is a concession as a right over land (where no option to tax has been exercised) e.g. retail outlets (a licence to occupy).

(see **Chapter 5 Land & Property**)

Conferences, exhibitions and related facilities or services
Supplies of conference, exhibition or related facilities services are standard-rated including the provision of lecturers and speakers, the organisation of exhibitions or displays or the hiring of space or other accommodation for conferences or exhibitions (where an option to tax has been exercised).

Supplies of conference, exhibition or related facilities services are exempt in relation to the organisation of educational or professional conferences (e.g. for Continuing Professional Development) or seminars as an eligible body (see *VAT Notice 701/30 Education & Vocational Training*) or the hiring of space or other accommodation for conferences or exhibitions (where no option to tax has been exercised).

(see **Chapter 5 Land & Property**)

Construction, alteration, demolition, repair or maintenance work, civil engineering
Work, Any Related Services or Goods

(see **Chapter 5 Land & Property**)

Contract or procurement services
Supplies of contract or procurement services are standard-rated.

Copying or supply of any reproductions or documents
Supplies of extracts from books, booklets, pamphlets, leaflets, second or additional copies of patients' notes or X-rays supplied to solicitors, insurers or other external organisations or the use of photocopiers or other reprographic equipment are standard-rated.

Supplies of books, booklets, pamphlets, leaflets, brochures, newspapers, magazines, journals, periodicals are zero-rated.

Copyright, patents or licences to manufacture
Supplies of copyright, patents or licences to manufacture are standard-rated.

Delivery or distribution services
Supplies of delivery or distribution services are standard-rated.

Drainage work
Supplies of drainage works or services are standard-rated (see **Chapter 5 Land & Property**).

Electronic transfer of data
Supplies of the electronic transfer of data are standard-rated.

Export of goods and related services
(see **Chapter 6 International VAT**)

Filming, replay or recording services
Supplies of film or recording services or similar are standard-rated.

Financial and any related services
Supplies of financial services are exempt (but related services such as administration and bookkeeping are standard-rated).

Fishing licences or permits
Supplies of fishing licences or permits are normally standard-rated. Supplies of fishing licences or permits are sporting right i.e. the right to take game or fish from land. The supply of sporting rights is normally standard-rated. However, if the sporting rights form part of a supply of land, there are occasions when the liability of the sporting rights will follow the liability of that land (i.e. exempt or standard-rated). Finally, in certain circumstances if there is a separate charge for fish taken then that may be zero-rated.

Fire service assistance
Supplies of fire service assistance are standard-rated.

Freight transport
Supplies of freight transport services are standard-rated.

BUSINESS ACTIVITIES

Fuel and power
Supplies of non-domestic fuel are standard-rated and supplies of domestic fuel are reduced-rate.

Government car service
Supplies of a government car service are standard-rated.

Grant or assignment or surrender of any interest in or right over land, or of any licence to do anything in relation to land
(see **Chapter 5 Land & Property**)

Grant of a right to inspect records
Supplies of a right to inspect records are standard-rated.

Goods, including goods manufactured within a government department and sold to its staff and to other customers, stores, surplus, or other equipment
Supplies of goods are standard-rated except where specifically reduced-rate or zero-rated (see **Appendix 7 Reduced-Rate Supplies** and **Appendix 8 Zero-Rated Supplies**). The liability of the supply may depend on the status of the recipient e.g. supplies of pharmaceuticals to charities (zero-rated).

Grave maintenance
Supplies of grave maintenance services are standard-rated.

Grounds maintenance
Supplies of grounds or garden maintenance services are standard-rated.

Hairdressing
Supplies of hairdressing for staff or the public are standard-rated.

Heating
Supplies of non-domestic fuel are standard-rated and supplies of domestic fuel are reduced-rate.

Hire of vehicles, machinery or equipment, with or without operator crew
The following supplies of the hire of vehicles, machinery or equipment, with or without operator crew are standard-rated:
- hire of a GD vehicle (designed or adapted to carry less than 10 passengers) with or without a driver e.g. cars
- hire of a GD vehicle (designed or adapted to carry less than 10 passengers) without a driver e.g. coaches or minibuses
- private use on hire of a GD vehicle (designed or adapted to carry less than 10 passengers) e.g. cars
- private use on hire of a GD vehicle (designed or adapted to carry less than 10 passengers) e.g. coaches or minibuses

- hire of GD machinery or equipment (with or without operator crew)

The following supplies of the hire of vehicles, machinery or equipment, with or without operator crew are zero-rated:
- hire of a GD vehicle (designed or adapted to carry not less than 10 passengers) with a driver e.g. coaches or minibuses

Passenger transport charges (e.g. by bus, rail, air or sea) are normally zero-rated. Where a GD supplies qualifying passenger transport services (e.g. a coach or minibus with a driver) that would be zero-rated but the hire of a GD vehicle without a driver would be standard-rated.

Hydrographic, cartographic and similar services
Supplies of hydrographic, cartographic and similar services are standard-rated.

Information or statistical services
Supplies of information or statistical services are standard-rated.

Charges made for the provision of information requested under the Freedom of Information Act 2000 is not treated as being a taxable supply provided that the information can only be provided by that specific GD and is not available from any other source (outside the scope of VAT).

Inspection services
Supplies of health and safety inspection services are standard-rated.

Laboratory services Including Analysis and Testing of Any Substance
The following supplies of laboratory services including analysis and testing of any substance are standard-rated:
- testing and analysis services when performed by a person not enrolled on a statutory medical register (see **Appendix 9 – Schedule 9 Group 7**)
- testing and analysis services when performed or supervised by a person enrolled on a statutory medical register (see **Appendix 9 – Schedule 9 Group 7**) and where the primary purpose of the service is not the protection, maintenance or restoration of the health of the person receiving the service;
- writing of scientific reports when performed by a person not enrolled on a statutory medical register (see **Appendix 9 – Schedule 9 Group 7**)
- writing of scientific reports when produced or supervised by a person enrolled on a statutory medical register (see **Appendix 9 – Schedule 9 Group 7**) and where the primary purpose of the service is not the protection, maintenance or restoration of the health of the person receiving the service;

- laboratory services (including X-ray services and analyses and the processing of urea) supplied by unqualified technicians working without supervision; and
- laboratory services (including X-ray services and analyses and the processing of urea) when performed or supervised by a person enrolled on a statutory medical register (see **Appendix 9 – Schedule 9 Group 7**) and where the primary purpose of the service is not the protection, maintenance or restoration of the health of the person receiving the service.

The following supplies of laboratory services including analysis and testing of any substance are exempt:

- testing and analysis services when performed or supervised by a person enrolled on a statutory medical register (see **Appendix 9 – Schedule 9 Group 7**) and where the primary purpose of the service is the protection, maintenance or restoration of the health of the person receiving the service;
- writing of scientific reports when produced or supervised by a person enrolled on a statutory medical register (see **Appendix 9 – Schedule 9 Group 7**) and where the primary purpose of the service is the protection, maintenance or restoration of the health of the person receiving the service; and
- laboratory services (including X-ray services and analyses and the processing of urea) when performed or supervised by a person enrolled on a statutory medical register (see **Appendix 9 – Schedule 9 Group 7**) and where the primary purpose of the service is the protection, maintenance or restoration of the health of the person receiving the service.

Laundry services
Supplies of laundry services are standard-rated e.g. to staff or an external organisation or business.

Licensing, certification, authorisation or the granting of any rights other than rights over land
Supplies of grants of Crown Copyright or software licences are standard-rated supplies of services.

Manufacturing, assembling and other services
Supplies of manufactured products e.g. during industrial or occupational therapy, are standard-rated.

Medical services

Supplies of medical services are exempt when performed or supervised by a person enrolled on a statutory medical register and where the primary purpose of the service is the protection, maintenance or restoration of the health of the person receiving the service:

- medical practitioners (including with limited registration)
- ophthalmologic opticians or dispensing opticians
- osteopaths or chiropractors
- qualified nurses and midwifes
- dispensers of hearing aids
- dentists, dental auxiliaries and dental technicians
- pharmaceutical chemists

Membership subscriptions

The liability of membership subscriptions reflects the benefit(s) members receive in return.

There may be a principal benefit and therefore a single supply with a single VAT liability (i.e. that of the principal benefit) or there may be a multiple supply and an apportionment will be necessary to reflect the different liabilities of different components of the supply. Membership benefits can be standard-rated, zero-rated, exempt or, in certain circumstances, non-business.

Non-profit making bodies (e.g. charities) making a single supply which comprises a mixture of benefits with different VAT liabilities are allowed to apportion their subscriptions to reflect the value and VAT liability of each individual benefit.

(see *VAT Notice 701/5 Clubs & Associations*)

Meteorological and related services

Supplies of weather forecasts or the provision of data relating to weather or climate change, or the use of computer modelling to simulate weather conditions or climate change are standard-rated supplies of services.

Mortuary services

Supplies of mortuary services, storage of remains and post-mortem examinations are standard-rated.

A post-mortem carried out under Coroners Act 1998 s.19 (i.e. an appointment by the coroner) is outside the scope of VAT.

BUSINESS ACTIVITIES

Nursery and daycare facilities
The provision of childcare or crèche/nursery services by a supplier not registered with OFSTED (under the Children Act 1989 as amended by the Care Standards Act 2000) is standard-rated.

The provision of childcare or crèche/nursery services by a supplier registered with OFSTED (under the Children Act 1989 as amended by the Care Standards Act 2000) is exempt.

Supplies of childcare or crèche/nursery services by an associated charity where charges are designed only to cover costs is outside the scope of VAT.

Occupational health services
The following supplies of occupational health services are standard-rated:
- manufactured goods or equipment e.g. from industrial or occupational therapy
- pre-employment medicals in relation to the health and medical fitness of the prospective employee
- post-employment medicals in relation to pension schemes
- ergonomic and risk assessments
- advice or helpline services
- counselling, lifestyle assessments, health and safety audits

The following supplies of occupational health services are zero-rated:
- food produce e.g. from industrial or occupational therapy

The following supplies of occupational health services are exempt:
- post-employment medicals in relation to the health and medical fitness of the employee
- post-employment training and advice to promote and maintain the health and medical fitness of employees

Passenger transport
The following supply of passenger transport is standard-rated:
- transport in any vehicle with driver or crew designed or adapted to carry less than 10 passengers e.g. taxis or private hire cars

The following supply of passenger transport is zero-rated:
- transport in any vehicle with driver or crew designed or adapted to carry not less than 10 passengers e.g. coaches or minibuses

Payroll and Pension Administration Services
Supplies of payroll or pension administration services, payment of salaries and wages, deductions from employees pay for insurance premiums, mortgage repayments, Trade Union subscriptions or in compliance with an attachment of earnings order.

Pest or animal control
Supplies of pest control or animal control services are standard-rated.

Photocopying services
The following supplies of photocopying services are standard-rated:
- extracts from books, booklets, pamphlets, leaflets
- second or additional copies of patients' notes or X-rays supplied to solicitors, insurers or other external organisations
- the use of photocopiers or other reprographic equipment

The following supplies of photocopying services are zero-rated:
- books, booklets
- pamphlets, leaflets, brochures
- newspapers, magazines, journals, periodicals

Photographic services
Supplies of photographic services are standard-rated.

Port, airport or harbour services and related goods
Supplies of services provided for the handling of ships or aircraft in a port, customs and excise airport or outside the UK are zero-rated. Includes salvage, pilotage and towage services. Also includes port and harbour dues, dock and berth charges, aircraft landing, parking and housing fees.

Postal, packing or distribution services
Supplies of postal services provided by the Royal Mail subject to a universal service obligation are exempt (excludes courier and parcel services).

Other postal, packing or distribution services that are not subject to a universal service obligation are standard-rated (including courier and parcel services).

Professional services including those of any manager, adviser, expert, specialist or consultant
Supplies of professional services are standard-rated including:
- legal, accounting, IT or computing, management, administration or other advisory or consultancy services
- medico-legal services including arbitration, mediation, conciliation and services provided to insurers or claimants, the preparation or consideration of medical reports in relation to claims or disputes
- scientific testing or analysis (e.g. drugs or materials)

The following supplies of professional services are exempt when performed by a person enrolled on a statutory medical register and where the primary purpose of the service is the protection, maintenance or restoration of the health of the person receiving the service:

- medical practitioners (including with limited registration)
- ophthalmologic opticians or dispensing opticians
- osteopaths or chiropractors
- qualified nurses and midwifes
- dispensers of hearing aids
- dentists, dental auxiliaries and dental technicians
- pharmaceutical chemists

Publications
The following supplies of publications are standard-rated:
- electronic publications e.g. ebooks, CDs, DVDs, microfilm, microfiche etc
- stationery e.g. letterheads, forms, cards, compliment slips, envelopes, invoices etc
- calendars, posters
- The following supplies of publications are zero-rated:
- books, booklets
- pamphlets, leaflets, brochures
- newspapers, magazines, journals, periodicals

Radio or communication services
Supplies of radio, communications or broadcasting services are standard-rated.

Recruitment services
Supplies of recruitment services are standard-rated.

Research, testing, experimentation, sampling or other related laboratory services
Supplies of research, testing, experimentation, sampling or other related laboratory services are standard-rated.

Supplies of research, testing, experimentation, sampling or other related laboratory services funded by grants or donations are non-business activities.

The exemption for research supplied between eligible bodies under VAT Act 1994 Schedule 9 Group 6 – Education was abolished on 1 August 2013.

Repair or maintenance of machinery, equipment or other goods
Supplies of repair or maintenance services for non-qualifying goods or equipment are standard-rated.

Supplies of repair or maintenance services for qualifying goods or equipment are zero-rated (see **Appendix 8 – Zero-Rated Supplies**).

Searches

Supplies of search services are standard-rated.

Secondment of staff for services obtainable from the private sector

If the recipient is not a GD then the secondment of staff is a standard-rated supply of staff. If the recipient is a GD the supply may either standard-rated or non-business. The supplying GD has to consider whether the services provided by the seconded employee could be obtained from the private sector. If the secondee could be obtained only from a GD, and not from the private sector, the supply is treated as being outside of the scope of VAT. This is because no distortion of competition can arise. The secondment of general administrators and directors will not fall under these provisions, as they will not be able to satisfy all the necessary criteria.

If the secondee could be appointed from the private sector the supply may be standard-rated unless the following concessionary treatment applies. If the recipient pays the relevant costs directly to the staff and third parties the supply is outside the scope of VAT provided that the recipient exercises exclusive control over the allocation and performance of the employee's duties during the period of the secondment and the GD does not derive any financial gain from the secondment, whether this comes directly from the secondment or through any other arrangements it may have with the recipient.

Advice Sheet 2 – Supplies of Staff

Advice Sheet 2 from *Guidance Notes for Government Departments* (Seventh Edition Issued: 19 July 2012) is reproduced below:

What are supplies of staff?

You make a supply of staff for VAT purposes if you provide to another person, for payment, the use of an individual who is contractually employed by you. This applies whether the terms of the individual's employment with you are set out in a formal contract or letter of appointment, or are on a less formal basis. The determining factor is that the staff are not contractually employed by your customer, but come under the direction of that company.

How can I tell the difference between a supply of staff and a supply of services?

If you make supplies of services, e.g. construction services, to another person but your staff continue to operate under your own direction, this is not a supply of staff, but is a supply of those services. This distinction is significant where the services may be zero-rated or exempt, or when determining whether or not the supply is made in the UK.

What happens when my department supplies staff to one of its Executive Agencies?

If the supplies are made to an Executive Agency that shares your VAT registration - no VAT is due on the supply. This is because the supply is taking place within the same legal entity.

If you are supplying staff to an Executive Agency that is separately registered for VAT, you will need to need to consider the guidance set out below.

What happens when a GD makes a supply of staff?

There are special rules that apply to supplies made by GD. If the supplies could only be obtained by a GD then no VAT is due, whereas if the supplies could be obtained from either a GD or the private sector, VAT will be applicable. These special rules are explained in more detail below. They ensure that where a supply could be obtained from either a GD or from the private sector, both supplies are treated in the same way. This is to recognise that supplies of certain staff between GDs do not distort competition with the private sector.

As such, when a department makes a supply of staff to another body it will need to consider whether the supply that is being made could also be obtained from the private sector.

How can I tell if a post could be filled from the private sector?

You need to consider whether there are specific skills or knowledge which are not available outside the Government sector.

Can you provide some examples of specialist posts?

Specialist posts are those in which the official has specific qualities/skills, which could not be obtained from the private sector or a job that just doesn't exist in the private sector, and can therefore only be done by a civil servant. This could include knowledge of specific departmental legislation, bespoke IT systems, procedures or security measures; where this knowledge is not in the public domain.

What should I do if the post can only be filled by a Civil Servant?

In circumstances where a GD supplies staff for a post that, by virtue of the work undertaken, can only be filled by a civil servant with the relevant specialist knowledge; VAT should not be charged. This is because the GD is the only possible source of the supply.

What should I do if the post can be filled by someone from the private sector?

In such cases, the VAT must be charged, unless the statement of practice relating to staff applies. (Please see below for more information). Where a taxable supply of staff takes place, VAT is due on the whole value of the consideration for the supply. In addition to any fee charged for the supply, the value of the consideration includes any reimbursement of salary costs, National Insurance and pension contributions.

More details on establishing the value of the supply of staff can be found in VAT Notice 700/34 "Staff"

What is the "statement of practice"?

The statement of practice applies if your customer pays the relevant costs directly to the staff and third parties. You may exclude these amounts from the taxable consideration for your supplies of staff provided -

- your customer exercises exclusive control over the allocation and performance of the employee's duties during the period of secondment; and
- your department does not derive any financial gain from the secondment, whether this comes directly from the secondment or through any other arrangements you may have with the recipient business - for example, from a management services agreement relating to the seconded staff.

It is important to remember that the amounts in question may only be disregarded from determining the consideration and value of the secondment when they are paid directly to the individual and/or third parties. If these amounts are received by you, they cannot be so disregarded and will be taken to be part of the consideration and value of the supply.

These rules apply whether you supply full-time or part-time staff. They also apply to the value of supplies received from outside the UK under the "reverse charge" procedure Please refer to VAT notice 741A" Place of Supply of Services" for more information.

The Statement of Practice refers to "exclusive control", what does this mean?

The term "exclusive control" refers to the extent to which the host organisation has control over the "day to day" activities of the employee who is being seconded/supplied to it.

In other words you will need to consider whether your department when acting as a supplier can impose restrictions on work areas/given tasks during the period that your employee is away on secondment. If your department GD imposes restrictions on the types of work your employee can be asked to do, then this does not meet the criteria for the statement of practice and your supply will be subject to VAT.

Examples where the host organisation will not have exclusive control over the secondee's day to day duties at their new location could include a situation where a GD stipulates that their employee does not work in specific areas as it could lead to a conflict of interests. This type of restriction is usually imposed to prevent the secondee working in areas where he/she has been privy to privileged information whilst a civil servant.

Please note that HMRC always expects that the parent GD would retain ultimate responsibility for the disciplinary matters and right to dismiss their employee. This ensures that Civil Servants remained fully accountable and

BUSINESS ACTIVITIES

abide by the accepted codes of conduct for their departments even when they are working in other GDs or outside bodies.

Aide Memoire for VAT treatment of Supplies of Staff

Stage No.	Things which need to be considered	VAT Treatment
Stage 1	In the first instance, you will need to establish whether your customer is a GD. You can do this by asking your customer for its VAT registration number. GDs have special VAT registration numbers which begin with the sequence 888 8 followed by two additional numbers	**If your customer *IS* a GD please move on to Stage 2** **If your customer is *NOT* a GD, please move on to stage 3**
Stage 2	You will then need to consider whether the services provided by the seconded employee could be obtained from the private sector. **a) If the secondee could be obtained only from a GD and not from private practice or the private sector** A simple way to establish whether the only source of supply is the GD is to consider how the secondment opportunity was originally advertised. Internal advertisements placed exclusively in departmental newsletters/circulars are an indication that the only possible source of the secondee could be a GD. You must also consider whether the secondment required specific **specialist knowledge** that could only come from someone inside a GD. **Please note** that the secondment of general administrators and Directors will NOT fall under these provisions, as they will not be able to satisfy all the necessary criteria set out above	**The supply is treated as being outside of the scope of VAT.** This is because no distortion of competition can arise.
Stage 2	**b) If the secondee could be appointed from the private sector-** the supply may be subject to VAT.	**The supply is standard rated unless the concession referred to in Stage 4 applies.**
Stage 3	If your customer is not a GD.	**The supply is most likely to be standard rated unless the concession referred**

		to in **Stage 4 applies.**
		In exceptional cases the supply may be treated as outside the scope if the only possible source of the secondee is from within government
Stage 4	Under the statement of practice , if your customer pays the relevant costs directly to the staff and third parties, the payment is not seen as a consideration for a supply provided that: - the customer **exercises exclusive** control over the allocation and performance of the employee's duties during the period of the secondment; and - the GD **does not derive any financial gain** from the secondment, whether this comes directly from the secondment or through any other arrangements which you may have with the customer. More information about this easement can be found in section B of The Appendices to **VAT notice 700/34 entitled "Staff".**	**Provided all the conditions set out in Part B of the Appendix to VAT notice 700/34 are satisfied, the reimbursement of salary costs are not seen as being a supply for VAT purposes. The payment is outside the scope of VAT and as such no VAT should be charged.**

Secretarial services
Supplies of secretarial services are standard-rated including typing services and the taking of minutes.

Transcription services
Supplies of transcription services are standard-rated.

Security services and related goods
Supplies of security services and related goods are standard-rated, including the provision of security guards, the installation of security systems such as door key pads, CCTV, security lighting etc.

Shipping services
Supplies of shipping services including the preparation of import/export documentation and allowing the use of freight containers are standard-rated.

However, these supplies are subject to the place of supply rules and depending on the status of the recipient (i.e. business or consumer) and the nature of the supply the place of supply may not be the UK and therefore the supply would be outside the scope of UK or, potentially, outside the scope of EU VAT altogether if performed for a recipient established outside the EU.

(see **Chapter 6 International VAT**)

Slaughter, rendering and disposal of animals
Supplies of the slaughter, rendering and disposal of animals are standard-rated.

Supplies of animal products for human consumption are zero-rated.

(see *VAT Notice 701/40 Food Processing Services*)

Social services
Supplies of social services are exempt including welfare services. Welfare services are defined as services directly connected with the provision of care, treatment or instruction designed to promote physical or mental welfare of elderly, distressed or disabled persons i.e. not medical care (see **Appendix 9 – Exempt Supplies**).

(see *VAT Notice 701/2 Welfare*)

Statistical services, including the collection, preparation and processing of data
Supplies of statistical services are standard-rated including the collection, preparation and processing of data, the preparation of statistical reports, medical or social surveys and statistical data processing.

Statistical services of themselves are standard-rated however if the services form part of a single (or composite) supply of research services the liability will follow that of the principal supply.

Storage facilities and related services
Supplies of storage or warehousing services are standard-rated.

Telecommunications
The liability of supplies of telecommunications are as follows:
- private use by employees (standard-rated);
- income from payphones including rented payphones (standard-rated)
- commission on payphones where an option to tax has been exercised (standard-rated);
- right over land e.g. for the siting of a mast where an option to tax has been exercised (standard-rated);

- commission on payphones where no option to tax has been exercised (exempt); and
- right over land e.g. for the siting of a mast (exempt).

Training, tuition or education and any related goods or services

The liability of supplies of training, tuition or education and any related goods or services provided by a GD as an eligible body is as follows:

- goods and services not closely related to education or not for the direct personal use of the student e.g. training CDs, DVDs (standard-rated);
- goods and services not closely related to education or not for the direct personal use of the student e.g. textbooks and training materials (zero-rated);
- education and vocational training including lectures, seminars, conferences and symposia (exempt);
- first aid courses, paramedic training and other medical training etc (exempt); and
- goods and services closely related to education and for the direct personal use of the student e.g. textbooks and training materials, accommodation, catering and transport (exempt).

Training and tuition when provided by an eligible body is an exempt supply and GDs qualify as eligible bodies. Supplies of goods and services essential to providing the training or tuition are also exempt as supplies closely related to education. (*VAT Notice 701/30 Education & Vocational Training*).

Transfer of milk quota leases

The transfer of a milk quota lease (without a corresponding right over land) is a standard-rated supply of services.

Translation services

Supplies of translation services are standard-rated, including the supply of oral interpreters or written translations.

Tree planting and afforestation

Supplies of tree planting, afforestation and forest management are standard-rated.

Vehicle conversions

Supplies of converting a vehicle for the personal use of a disabled individual are zero-rated.

Vehicle servicing and maintenance

Supplies are of vehicle servicing and maintenance services (including any parts supplied) are standard-rated.

BUSINESS ACTIVITIES

Supplies are of vehicle servicing and maintenance services for qualifying vehicles (including any parts supplied) are zero-rated (see **Appendix 8 – Zero-Rated Supplies**).

MOT Tests are outside the scope of VAT (but any repairs which require to be carried out to pass an MOT are standard-rated).

Verification of particulars of births, marriages or deaths
Supplies of duplicate copies of birth, death or marriage certificates or confirming information on application forms and other official forms are standard-rated.

Waste disposal
The following supplies of waste disposal services are standard-rated:
- incineration of waste products;
- removal, conveyance, treatment or disposal of the contents of cesspools, septic tanks or similar receptacles, where supplied to industrial customers; and
- removal of industrial waste not discharged into sewers.

The following supplies of waste disposal services are zero-rated:
- removal, conveyance, treatment or disposal of the contents of cesspools, septic tanks or similar receptacles, where supplied to non-industrial customers.

Water (supplies of water and ice)
The liability of supplies of water or ice is as follows:
- water or ice supplied to industrial users (standard-rated)
- water or ice supplied to non-industrial users is zero-rated
- mineral water or bottled water (standard-rated)
- ordinary water supplied in bottles as a drought alleviation or other emergency measure (zero-rated)
- distilled or deionised water and water of similar purity (standard-rated)

(see *VAT Notice 701/16 Water and Sewerage Services*)

Weighbridge services
Supplies of weighbridge services are standard-rated.

5 Land and Property

5.1 Introduction

The supply of land and property is one of the most complex areas of the tax because of the underlying complexity of property law (see *VAT Notice 742 Land & Property*). The tax position reflects the underlying legal position. Because of this it is always prudent to take VAT advice in relation to any property transaction in the same way that legal advice would be taken (i.e. when a lease is drafted or a sale proposed or as part of the planning process).

Under Schedule 9 Group 1 of VAT Act 1994 the grant of any interest in or right over land or of any licence to occupy land is exempt (see below). Where an option to tax is exercised by the taxpayer this supply becomes standard-rated but under current Treasury policy an option to tax may only be exercised by a GD in relation to a disposal of land or property and then only with the express permission of Treasury.

The main supplies of land and property as a business activity by GDs are:
- supplies of accommodation to other GDs or the NHS (exempt);
- supplies of accommodation to partnership organisations e.g. charities, higher educational institutions, further education colleges, local authorities, police and fire authorities (exempt);
- supplies of office or commercial accommodation to businesses e.g. leased offices or retail premises, serviced or unserviced (exempt);
- supplies of residential accommodation (exempt); and
- sales of land or property (exempt or standard-rated with Treasury permission).

Therefore where a GD rents out or leases property or grants a licence to occupy for a consideration there will be an exempt supply. This means that none of the VAT incurred on costs attributable to the exempt supply of land or property is recoverable either as input tax or COS and in relation to land or property these sums can be significant.

5.2 The Legal Context

VAT in the UK is ultimately governed by EU law (the *Principal VAT Directive 2006/112/EC*) though all Member States enact their own legislation interpreting the Directive (known as indirect effect). Where there is a conflict UK law is subordinate to EU law (although UK taxpayers are entitled to rely on domestic law until it is changed). In the UK the primary legislation is the Value Added Tax Act 1994 although there are various other Statutory Instruments and Regulations (notably the *VAT Regulations*

1995 SI 1995/2518) collectively known as secondary legislation. In addition, some HMRC publications have the force of law and amendments are regularly made via the annual Finance Acts (changes to secondary legislation can be made at any time).

The main sources of VAT law relating to land and property are:

The VAT Act 1994:
- Schedule 9 Group 1 – exempt supplies
- Schedule 8 Groups 5 & 6 – zero-rated supplies
- Schedule 7A Groups 2, 3, 6 & 7– reduced-rate supplies
- Schedule 10 – buildings and land

5.3 Supplies of Land & Property

5.3.1 Exempt supplies

The grant of any interest in or right over land, any licence to occupy land or a personal right (in Scotland) is exempt, including sales of land or buildings, the leasing or letting of land or buildings or the sub-leasing or sub-letting of land or buildings.

An interest in land includes a legal interest, a beneficial interest, rights of entry, easements, wayleaves and profits à prendre (although these can also be standard-rated or zero-rated). A licence to occupy means a written or oral agreement for the leasing or letting of immoveable property but falling short of a formal lease for an agreed duration in return for payment the right to occupy a defined area (and exclude others from enjoying that right). The definitions of an interest in or right over land and licence to occupy are important because if a supply falls outside of these it will necessarily be standard-rated irrespective of any option to tax.

An example of a licence to occupy is the provision of office accommodation in return for a monthly rent with the right to use shared areas such as reception, lifts, tea points and rest rooms. The predominant supply is the right to occupy defined office accommodation and exclude others. The fact that the licensee may have to share other parts of the building does not affect the occupational rights granted by the licence. This means that the supply is exempt unless an option to tax is exercised.

Another example is a specified area of office space less than a complete floor or room, such as a bank of desks in return for a periodic licence fee. A licence to occupy land can be granted in respect of parts of rooms and floors and consequently can exist within an open plan office area. The important point here is that there has to be an identifiable area of land that the licensee has an exclusive right to occupy during the period of the licence or the times specified in the licence (occupation does not have to be continuous).

Other examples include specified areas of storage space within a building, such as a room, cupboard or marked area for which someone is granted exclusive use or a catering concession where the caterer is granted a licence to occupy a specific kitchen and restaurant area, or the right to run a landfill site to an operator from a specified area of land, or the hiring of a hall or other accommodation for meetings, parties, etc (including use of kitchen area, lighting, furniture, etc). Most supplies of hiring out such accommodation will constitute a licence to occupy land. Access to kitchens, toilets, car parking etc is incidental to the predominant supply of land. However, if other services, such as catering, are provided the supply is likely to be a standard rated supply of services.

5.3.2 Standard-rated supplies

The grant of any interest in or right over land, any licence to occupy land or a personal right (in Scotland) is standard-rated where an option to tax has been granted (but the option to tax is disapplied in relation to residential or charitable use) including sales of land or buildings, the leasing or letting of land or buildings or the sub-leasing or sub-letting of land or buildings.

The grant or assignment of the freehold interest in a non-qualifying building (i.e. a commercial building) which has not been completed, a new building which is not to be used as qualifying building after the grant (completed less than three years before the grant) or civil engineering works (e.g. roads, tunnels and bridges) which have not been completed or a new civil engineering work is standard-rated (completed less than three years before the grant). Other standard-rated supplies of property include hotel, holiday (and similar) accommodation, recreational caravans and camping pitches, parking facilities, storage facilities, and gaming and fishing rights, boxes and seats at sporting events or theatres etc, and sports facilities, except where there is a series of at least 10 bookings (exempt).

Hotel and holiday accommodation includes accommodation a hotel, inn, boarding house or similar establishment (including short-term lets and serviced apartments) and includes furnished sleeping accommodation. Where guests stay for a continuous period of four weeks more a reduced rate applies. Also includes chalets, cottages, huts etc, seasonal caravan and tent pitches (i.e. non-residential) but not rented residential accommodation in a caravan or mobile home (exempt). Parking facilities include the grant or assignment of facilities for parking a vehicle, the letting or licensing of garages, the letting, licensing or provision of taxi ranks, bicycle storage, rights to park vehicles, purpose-built car parks and the sale of new or partly competed garages etc.

5.3.3 Zero-rated supplies

The first grant of a major interest in a qualifying building (residential or for charitable non-business use) by a person constructing the building is zero-rated. The first grant of a major interest in a protected building which has been substantially reconstructed by a person reconstructing the building is zero-rated. A qualifying building is one which is designed as a dwelling or a number of dwellings or intended for use for a relevant charitable purpose (at least 95% non-business by concession) or intended for a relevant residential purpose (the main residence of at least 90% of the residents). The first grant includes the first sale or long lease but excludes any second or subsequent long lease or any sale after leasing it on a long lease. In England, Wales and Northern Ireland a major interest means the fee simple or a tenancy for a term certainly exceeding 21 years and in Scotland the interest of the owner or a lessee under a lease for a period of not less than 20 years. In England and Wales the fee simple means the freehold and in Scotland the fee simple means the interest of the owner.

5.3.4 Non-business activities

Non-business activities are activities outside the scope of VAT which are not carried on for a business purpose including charitable activities and the statutory duties of GDs. From 1 January 2011 these are included in the £250,000 value for the purposes of the Capital Goods Scheme.

5.3.5 Accounting for VAT

Output tax is due on taxable supplies of land or property. Input tax is allowable on the direct and indirect costs attributable to taxable supplies of land or property.

There are three levels of input tax recovery related to supplies of land or property:

- **direct recovery** on directly attributable input tax – such as VAT incurred on construction, demolition, site clearance, professional fees, peripheral works, maintenance costs, utilities or any other cost directly attributable to the taxable supply etc.
- **indirect recovery** on sectorised costs such as the administration of estates and facilities or leased accommodation. Further calculations will be necessary to determine this proportion, but typically it would be based on a floorspace analysis and ratio. This percentage is then applied to the sectorised costs and that proportion of the VAT incurred is allowable input tax.

- **residual recovery** on general overheads. In this context the residual input tax entitlement arises as a proportion of VAT incurred on general non-attributable overheads for the organisation as a whole. Any one-off sales or purchases of land or property should be excluded as incidental. Therefore, the residual input tax entitlement will normally only arise in relation to ongoing supplies of land or property such as leased accommodation (any VAT incurred on costs which has been taken into account above should be excluded).

Input tax entitlement arises in relation to taxable supplies made or intended to be made irrespective of the type of supply. The amount of input tax allowable will depend on the proportion of the VAT incurred which relates or will relate to taxable supplies. Further calculations will be necessary to determine this proportion in each project, but typically it would be based on a floorspace analysis and ratio (excluding the common areas of buildings which are non-attributable). From 1 January 2011 any capital project with a net value in excess of £250,000 and including a business element (taxable or exempt) falls within the Capital Goods Scheme.

5.4   Sales of Land & Buildings

Except in relation to the sale of a commercial building which is less than three years old (standard-rated) when a GD sells land or buildings there will normally be an exempt supply. If the option to tax is exercised the supply is standard-rated. If standard-rated output tax would be chargeable on the full value of the supply (and any Stamp Duty Land Tax payable on the transaction would be charged on the gross value). But an option to tax is normally advisable for the supplier because it gives rise to full input tax entitlement and all of the VAT incurred on costs attributable to the taxable supply of land or property is recoverable. Conversely, if the supply is not taxed and remains exempt none of the VAT incurred on costs attributable to the exempt supply of land or property is recoverable either as input tax or COS. In relation to sales of land or property the amount of input tax can be significant. GDs require Treasury permission to opt to tax the sale or disposal of a property but it should always be considered as there are significant benefits.

For example, the VAT on demolition and site clearance costs would be recoverable as input tax where an option to tax is exercised (and these costs are not eligible for COS recovery). VAT on legal fees and other professional fees is not recoverable as COS in relation to an exempt supply even where the ultimate purpose of the transaction is the non-business activity of a GD. The rule in relation to input tax or COS recovery is that for direct attribution there must be a direct and immediate link to the supply or activity. Therefore, VAT incurred where there is a direct and immediate link to an exempt supply will not be allowable input tax or eligible for COS recovery, but if the transaction is taxed all of the VAT incurred is allowable input tax.

5.5   The Option to Tax

The option to tax is a provision which allows a taxable person to tax certain supplies of land, buildings or property which would otherwise be exempt (land includes any buildings or structures permanently affixed). Because these supplies are now taxable this creates an entitlement to claim credit for allowable input tax attributable to taxable supplies.

The effect of the option to tax is that VAT must be charged on all future supplies related to the opted property by the person opting unless blocked by an anti-avoidance provision or the option has been revoked. The option remains effective even where the person opting deregisters due to a fall in turnover but then has to re-register. If at any time a grant is made in relation to the land or property by the person opting (or a relevant associate) when the option to tax has effect then the supply is standard-rated. Grant includes an assignment or surrender and the supply made by the person to whom an interest is surrendered when there is a reverse surrender.

The option to tax applies to the person making the option in relation to specified land, buildings or property. The person opting does not have to own the opted land, buildings or property and only supplies made by the person opting are affected (i.e. the option to tax does not transfer).

For example:
- a person who purchases a building where an option to tax has been exercised by the purchaser is not obliged to opt to tax or charge output tax on any subsequent lets or disposal;
- a person who sub-lets a property may opt to tax their sub-let even where they are not charged VAT on the principal supply; but
- in practice, an option will follow an option to reclaim input tax.

The option applies:
- in relation to a building it applies to the whole of the building and all land within its curtilage;
- to land under and immediately around the building (including forecourts and yards); but
- *not* to a separate car park;

- in relation to land it covers all land and any buildings or civil engineering works on the land;

From 1 June 2008 if a building is demolished or destroyed any option still applies to the land and to any future building constructed on the land and if a new building is constructed on opted land it is covered by the option unless HMRC are notified that the building is to be excluded from the option. Real estate elections were introduced in 2008 as a formal decision to opt to tax all future property acquisitions. Each property is treated as separately opted (and therefore may be separately revoked). The person opting is treated as having exercised the option on the day the acquisition was made in relation to any relevant interest in land or property.

There are two stages in opting to tax:
(1) making the decision to opt to tax; and
(2) notifying HMRC of the decision to opt to tax.

A written record should be kept of the decision to opt and HMRC should be notified within 30 days of the option taking effect. HMRC permission is required where there have been previous exempt supplies (and notification is thus not required). Automatic permission is granted where the only input tax to be reclaimed is incurred after the option takes effect and relates to general maintenance and overheads otherwise written permission is required from HMRC. HMRC must be satisfied that there will be a fair and reasonable attribution of input tax to taxable supplies.

If notification is late HMRC has discretion to accept belated notifications although they cannot grant retrospection and will generally accept these where there is evidence that a genuine decision was taken to opt to tax but it has not been notified in time. They may refuse a belated notification if acceptance would produce an unfair result or in relation to an avoidance scheme. The option to tax is disapplied in in relation to residential property, or in relation to non-business activities or a relevant charitable purpose (but not charity offices), or in relation to grants made to relevant housing associations in relation to residential property and in relation to DIY housebuilders. Finally, there are limited circumstances in which an option to tax can be revoked. It can be revoked by the taxpayer in a six month cooling off period or automatically where no interest has been held in the land or property for six years or by the taxpayer where more than 20 years have elapsed since the option first took effect.

(see *VAT Notice 742A Option to Tax*)

5.6   The Capital Goods Scheme

The Capital Goods Scheme is a form of extended partial exemption. From 1 January 2011 the Capital Goods Scheme includes non-business activities, and ships and aircraft and applies to land where the owner incurs VAT bearing capital expenditure of £250,000 or over on its acquisition, or a building or part of a building where the owner incurs VAT bearing capital expenditure of £250,000 or over on its acquisition, construction, refurbishment, fitting out, alteration or extension, or a civil engineering work or part of a civil engineering work where the owner incurs VAT bearing capital expenditure of £250,000 or over on its acquisition, construction, refurbishment, fitting out, alteration or extension.

The purpose of the scheme is to separate higher value projects from the general business/non-business and partial exemption calculations to achieve a more accurate attribution of input tax to taxable supplies. Only the proportion of the input tax attributable to taxable supplies can be reclaimed. An apportionment to determine the proportion of exempt supplies, taxable supplies (and non-business activities) is necessary. The scheme does not apply if assets are just acquired for resale, or there is expenditure on assets acquired just for resale, or assets are acquired (or there is expenditure on assets) that are only used for non-business purposes.

The £250,000 includes all of the costs in making the building ready including professional and managerial costs. VAT incurred after the first interval can be incorporated into the calculation. If VAT is incurred before the first interval a calculation is required to work out the overall initial percentage which can be claimed against which the percentage of taxable use in any subsequent interval can be measured.

The adjustment period for land, buildings or civil engineering works is 10 successive (annual) intervals. From 1 January 2011 the first interval commences on the day on which the owner first uses the capital item and ends on the day before the start of the next partial exemption tax year and thereafter at annual intervals. Subsequent intervals follow annually at the end of the partial exemption tax year. These are included in the second VAT period after the interval ends (which is the VAT period after the partial exemption annual adjustment).

The calculation is based on the annual variation from the baseline percentage of taxable use. The baseline percentage is the taxable percentage at the end of the first interval. At each (annual) interval thereafter the taxable percentage is calculated and if there is a variation from the baseline there is an adjustment. The final adjustment is made in the normal way in the tenth interval and no further adjustments are required. If there is a change of use after the final adjustment it is disregarded.

If there is a transfer of a going concern the purchaser is treated as the owner of the capital item and is also treated as having done everything done by the seller. In the case of a VAT Group the representative member is treated as the owner and as having everything done by a group member in respect of the asset. If a capital item is disposed of before the end of the adjustment period the interval in which it is disposed of is treated as the final interval. If it is disposed of before the end of the adjustment period HMRC may apply the disposal test. If the total input tax exceeds the output tax due on the disposal then it may be necessary to adjust the amount of input tax recovered in relation to the capital item.

(see *VAT Notice 706/2 Capital Goods Scheme*)

5.7   Anti-Avoidance Provisions

Some businesses whose supplies are wholly or partly exempt are not entitled to recover all of the input tax they incur on the purchase of land or buildings, or on major construction projects. As a result, some of these organisations entered into arrangements designed to either increase the amount of input tax they could claim, or to spread the VAT cost of the purchase or construction over a number of years. To counter this, an anti-avoidance test was introduced. The test is applied each time a grant is made and if caught, the option to tax will not have effect (it will be 'disapplied') in respect of the supplies that arise from that particular grant. The anti-avoidance test may also impact on the VAT treatment of a transfer of a going concern (TOGC) of a property.

If an interest is granted in a building or land and the person that is to be in occupation makes predominantly taxable supplies and is able to receive credit for the majority of input tax they incur the anti-avoidance measure is unlikely to apply. An option to tax may, however, be disapplied if any of the following situations arise:

- a business is partly exempt and grants a lease in a building that it intends to occupy at a later date;
- a business is partly exempt and enters into a sale and leaseback of a property that it occupies; a business constructs a building and finance is provided by a bank that also intends to be in occupation; or
- a business purchases a building and finance is provided by a bank that also intends to be in occupation.

Where supplies of property become exempt supplies due to the disapplication of an option to tax, this may mean that a business cannot recover input tax, or that it has to repay input tax that it has previously recovered.

5.7.1 The anti-avoidance test

If at the time of the grant of land or buildings the property is, or is expected to become, a capital item for the purposes of the Capital Goods Scheme, either for the grantor, a person to whom the property is transferred or a person treated as the grantor, and it is the intention or expectation of the grantor or the person treated as the grantor or a person responsible for financing the grantor's acquisition or development, that the building will be occupied by them or a person connected with them, and the person occupying the property will be doing so other than wholly or substantially wholly for eligible purposes, then the option to tax will not have effect in respect of supplies that arise from that particular grant.

There are several key elements to the test which potentially trigger the anti-avoidance provision:

- the property must be a capital item;
- there must be occupation of the property (either by the business or a connected person);
- there must be exempt supplies or non-business activities.

In effect, the option to tax is only blocked where the property is a capital item and it is used or occupied by a business or a connected person to make exempt supplies (for example, it does not affect supplies to an unconnected third party). Occupation wholly or substantially wholly for eligible purposes means for at least 80% taxable purposes or by a GD or other public bodies for at least 80% taxable or non-business purposes. The anti-avoidance provision still applies to GDs and other public bodies if the occupation is for the purpose of making exempt supplies but typically this means that a GD or other public body is not blocked from opting to tax part of a building where it is in occupation in respect of its non-business activities as a public body.

5.7.2 Occupation

A person is in occupation of a building or land if they have a physical presence, and the right to occupy the property as if they are the owner. This means they will have actual possession and control of the land, together with the ability to exclude others from the enjoyment of such rights. From 1 March 2011 a person in occupation of the land or building is treated as if he is not in occupation if the percentage occupied does not exceed 2% where the person is (or is connected with) the grantor, or the percentage occupied does not exceed 10% where the person is (or is connected with) a development financier (but not also (or connected with) the grantor).

Normally a legal interest in, or licence to occupy, the land will have been granted to them. However, occupation could also be by agreement or de facto and it is therefore necessary to take into account the day-to-day arrangements, particularly where these differ from the contractual terms. An exclusive right of occupation is not a requirement; an agreement might, for example, allow for joint occupation. It is also not necessary for a person to be utilising all of the land for all of the time for them to be considered as occupying it.

Businesses, such as insurance companies and banks, or educational institutions such as universities or further education colleges making exempt supplies, or someone who is not, and is not required to be VAT registered are examples of businesses and organisations that may occupy a property for other than eligible purposes and organisations, such as charities, which undertake non-business activities, would not generally be in occupation for eligible purposes.

5.7.3   Grantor & grant

The grantor is the person who sells, leases, licences or lets any of the land or buildings and the grant is the act that transfers the interest in, or possession of, the land or building e.g. a freehold sale of land or a building, the leasing or licensing of land or a building, or the assignment or surrender of that lease or licence. The word 'grant' refers to the act that transfers the interest in, or possession of, the land or building. Examples are a freehold sale of land or a building, the leasing or licensing of land or a building, or the assignment or surrender of that lease or licence. The grantor is the person who sells, leases, licences or lets any of the land or buildings. The test should be applied to each grant made.

5.7.4   Development financier

A person is deemed to have been responsible for financing an acquisition or development if two key conditions are met: at the time the finance is provided, or the agreement to provide the finance is entered into, the person providing the finance must intend or expect that he or the grantor, or somebody connected to either of them, will occupy the particular property for other than eligible purposes and the funds must be for the purpose of financing the purchase, construction or refurbishment of that property. If either of these conditions is not met, a person will not be deemed to be responsible for providing finance, even if he has provided the funds to meet part or all of the cost of the acquisition or development.

5.7.5 Connected persons

The test in the Corporation Tax Act 2010 s.1122 applies to determine whether persons are connected. The following persons are treated as connected:

- husband, wife or civil partner; relatives and their husbands, wives or civil partners; husband's, wife's or civil partner's relatives and their husbands, wives or civil partners;
- in a partnership, the partners and their husbands, wives, civil partners and relatives;
- a controlled company either by an individual or with any of the persons listed above; or
- for a settlor the trustees of a settlement, or of which a person who is still alive and who is connected is a settlor.

Relative means a brother, sister, ancestor or lineal descendant. It does not include nephews, nieces, uncles and aunts.

A company is connected with another company if the same person has control of both, or a person has control of one and persons connected with him (or he and persons connected with him) have control of the other, or if a group of two or more persons have control of each company, and the groups either consist of the same persons or could be regarded as consisting of the same persons by treating (in one or more cases) a member of either group as replaced by a person with whom he is connected. For the purposes of the option to tax a company is not treated as "connected" to another company as a result of both being under the control of:

- the Crown;
- a Minister of the Crown;
- a GD; or
- a Northern Ireland GD.

(see *Notice 742A Option to Tax*)

5.8 Landlord & Tenant

Where there is a supply of accommodation it is likely that there will be an associated supply of services. Again the complexity of the tax position reflects the underlying complexity of property law. The principal liabilities are set out here but it is prudent to take tax advice should when entering into any contract or rental agreement with tenants particularly when these involve inducements, reverse premiums, variations, surrenders, reverse surrenders, dilapidation payments or indemnity payments (with or without associated services – see *VAT Notice 742 Land & Property* for further details).

Rental or lease payments for domestic tenants is exempt and also exempt for non-domestic tenants unless an option to tax is exercised in which case standard-rated. Any option to tax would disapplied for domestic tenants. Rent free periods or inducements are generally outside the scope of VAT unless a taxable benefit is provided in return such as repairs and maintenance or reciprocal services. The liability of subsequent supplies under a lease is determined when the supply is made, rather by reference to the original grant, and where there is a variation of the lease there is no supply if the variation merely extends the term or the right of occupation. Surrenders of leases follow the liability of the main supply as do reverse surrenders. Rent adjustments between landlords on the sale of tenanted property are outside the scope of VAT as are rent adjustments between tenants on the assignment of a lease.

Any option to tax is disapplied in relation to residential property and disapplied in relation to non-business activities or a relevant charitable purpose. The option applies to the person making the option in relation to specified land, buildings or property but only supplies made by the person opting are affected. For example, a person who sub-lets a non-domestic property may opt to tax their sub-let even where they are not charged VAT on the principal supply. As a matter of Treasury policy GDs are not allowed to opt to tax supplies of commercial property but may well be charged VAT by a private landlord where commercial accommodation is leased from the private sector.

A managing agent acting on behalf of a landlord can treat general services charges to tenants as exempt but a managing agent acting on behalf of residents must treat general services charges to tenants as standard-rated (and the same principles apply to tenant-controlled management companies). An award of mesne profits is not consideration for a supply and is therefore outside the scope of VAT as are dilapidation payments and statutory compensation.

5.8.1   Non-domestic service charges

The liability of services provided by landlords for non-domestic property are as follows:

Service Charges – general services provided as part of a lease follow the liability of the main supply of accommodation – typically a service or maintenance charge connected with the external fabric or common areas or parts of the building (as opposed to demised areas of the property for individual occupants) – and paid for by all the occupants through a common service charge (**exempt**).

Insurance – if the landlord is the policyholder then the insurance payment from the tenant to the landlord is part payment for the main supply of accommodation and follows the liability of the main supply (**exempt**).

Insurance – if the tenant is the policyholder then the insurance payment from the tenant to the landlord and then paid by the landlord on behalf of the tenant is a disbursement and therefore outside the scope of VAT (**non-business**).

Rates – if the landlord is the rateable person then the rates payment from the tenant to the landlord is part payment for the main supply of accommodation and follows the liability of the main supply (**exempt**).

Rates – if the tenant is the rateable person then the rates payment from the tenant to the landlord and then paid by the landlord on behalf of the tenant is a disbursement and therefore outside the scope of VAT (**non-business**).

Telephones – if the account is in the name of the landlord then any charge for telephones by the landlord is a payment for a supply of services (**standard-rated**).

Telephones – if the account is in the name of the tenant then any payment from the tenant to the landlord and then paid by the landlord on behalf of the tenant is a disbursement and therefore outside the scope of VAT (**non-business**).

Reception/Switchboard – an inclusive charge under the lease for reception or switchboard facilities is part payment for the main supply of accommodation and follows the liability of the main supply (**exempt**).

Office Services – an inclusive charge under the lease for office services or facilities is part payment for the main supply of accommodation and follows the liability of the main supply (**exempt**).

Office Services – a separate charge for office services or facilities is a payment for a supply of services (**standard-rated**).

Fixtures & Fittings – an inclusive charge under the lease for fixtures and fittings is part payment for the main supply of accommodation and follows the liability of the main supply (**exempt**).

Fixtures & Fittings – a separate charge for fixtures and fittings is a payment for a supply of goods (**standard-rated**).

Utilities – a separate charge for un-metered supplies of fuel and power is treated as an additional payment for the main supply of accommodation and follows the liability of the main supply (**exempt**).

Utilities – a separate charge where the landlord operates secondary credit meters is payment for a supply of fuel and power (**standard-rated for non-domestic premises**).

Management Charges – a separate charge for the management of a development or administering the collection of services charges is treated as an additional payment for the main supply of accommodation and follows the liability of the main supply (**exempt**).

(see *VAT Notice 742 Land & Property*)

5.8.2 Domestic service charges

The liability of services provided by landlords for domestic residential property are as follows (except where provided to staff under a Whitley Council Agreement at a subsidised and uneconomic rent (non-business)):

Service Charges – mandatory services related to the upkeep of common areas on an estate of dwellings or the common areas of multi-occupied dwelling (**exempt**).

Service Charges – service charges provided separately or independently of the main supply of residential accommodation (**standard-rated**).

Utilities – a separate charge for un-metered supplies of fuel and power is treated as an additional payment for the main supply of residential accommodation (**exempt**).

Utilities – a separate charge where the landlord operates secondary credit meters is payment for a supply of fuel and power (**reduced-rate**).

(see *VAT Notice 742 Land & Property*)

5.8.3 Advice Sheet 4 – Land & Property

Advice Sheet 4 in relation to leased accommodation from *Guidance Notes for Government Departments* (Seventh Edition Issued: 19 July 2012) is reproduced below:

What do GDs do about leases and MOTO arrangements and what is the difference between them?

A lease is a commercial arrangement between a landlord and a tenant under a commercial leasing arrangement.

MOTO stands for Memorandum of Terms of Occupation. Many GDs occupy a building under a Memorandum of Terms of Occupation (MOTO). A MOTO is an agreement between two GDs which allows them to share the costs of renting a building or part of a building from a private commercial landlord.

Standard Commercial Leases

What happens when a GD acts as a landlord?

If a GD acts as landlord and supplies a lease to another GD, this is not a MOTO arrangement. The supply made is of leased accommodation and it is exempt.

Although the Estate Services Guide issued by the Central Advice Unit of the Property Advisors to the Civil Estate (PACE) should be consulted for more information, H.M. Treasury has advised that GDs must not opt to tax a lease to a tenant, unless there are specific circumstances and these have been approved by HMRC and HMT prior to the option taking place (whether another GD or any other type of body). Information for GDs in England and Wales can be found on page 251 of the 3rd Edition issued in June 1999. GDs in Scotland should consult page 161 Edition 2 issued in February 2000.

This means the GD as landlord must not charge the tenant VAT and will not be able to recover VAT on goods and services purchased for this exempt supply. The level of the rent may be set to include irrecoverable VAT, but this must not be shown as VAT on the invoice. Your tenant cannot reclaim the irrecoverable VAT included in the invoice as Input Tax.

What happens when a GD is a tenant?
GDs may occupy buildings rented from commercial landlords or other GDs under the terms of a standard commercial lease. Such leases are exempt from VAT, unless the commercial landlord has opted to tax. GDs cannot recover VAT they incur on the rent of a building occupied for non-business purposes. In addition, a GD cannot recover the VAT on a service charge that is part of the rent.

It is also important to remember that VAT incurred on buildings which are leased from commercial landlords cannot be recovered under heading 53 of the Contracting-Out Directions.

Opting to tax
As stated above GDs are not normally able to opt to tax supplies of land and buildings unless they are selling the property in question and then only with the specific permission of HM Treasury. Any such request should be submitted through your CRM or Customer Coordinator.

Information on opting to tax is found in VAT Notice 742A "Opting to tax land and buildings".

PFI - Public Finance Initiatives
A PFI company provides GDs with fully serviced and managed accommodation. The most distinct element of PFI arrangements is that risk is transferred from the GD to the PFI provider.

When a GD enters into a PFI arrangement for accommodation it will use for its non-business activities, VAT can be recovered under heading 53 of the Treasury's (Contracting Out) Directions.

What about recovery of VAT under MOTO Arrangements?
Treasury paper PES (99)23 dated 24 September 1999 gives guidance on recovery of VAT on civil estate leases.

The GD which has entered into the lease with the commercial landlord is known as the "Major Occupier".

The GD which agrees to share costs is known as the "Minor Occupier"

Under a MOTO, the major occupier is responsible for all VAT payments and for recovery of VAT. Generally MOTO arrangements fall into three distinct categories.

(a) Non-business activities where VAT is recoverable.
If a major occupier uses a building for its non-business activities, it can only recover VAT on those contracted-out services detailed in List 2 of the Contracting-Out Directions. If the major occupier is able to recover VAT it should ask the minor occupier for a VAT- exclusive contribution towards costs.

(b) Non-Business activities where VAT is not recoverable.
If the major occupier is not able to recover VAT, it may ask the Minor Occupier for a VAT-inclusive contribution towards its costs. Under the terms of the MOTO, the major occupier is not making a supply to the minor occupier. So, no VAT invoice should be issued and no VAT should be charged.

(c) Business activities.
If the major occupier provides a service to the minor occupier that is over and above what is in the MOTO this is a business activity of the major occupier who should charge the minor occupier VAT as appropriate.

Aide Memoire
Can my department recover the VAT it is charged on rents?

If the building is used for ...	Can VAT be recovered?
Standard-rated business activities	Input tax can be reclaimed under the normal VAT rules
Exempt business activities	Input tax cannot be recovered
Government Non-business activities	If a building is occupied under a normal commercial lease granted by a landlord, any VAT charged on the rents and service charges cannot be recovered under section 41(3). Most rents and service charges are exempt from VAT, but the landlord is entitled to "opt to tax" them at the standard rate of VAT. If you occupy the building under a PFI or similar arrangement - you may claim a refund of VAT under Heading 53 of the Treasury's (Contracting-Out) Directions.
More than one type of use.	The VAT must be apportioned between the business (taxable and exempt) and non-business uses – as mentioned above. Recovery of VAT is determined by how the building is used - see the section on purchases above.

Other sources of advice:
VAT Notice 742 "Land & Property" contains more information on general land & property issues.

Your CRM or Customer Coordinator can provide more information about the VAT Treatment of supplies of accommodation made to GDs.

5.9   Construction Services

The liability of construction services depends on the type of building works undertaken and the status of the person constructing the building i.e. whether the building is commercial, residential or charitable and whether the person constructing the building or carrying out the works is a developer, a main contractor or a subcontractor.

For the purposes of reduced-rating or zero-rating a qualifying building is a building which is designed as a dwelling or a number of dwellings or is intended for use solely for a relevant charitable purpose (95% non-business use by concession) or intended for use solely for a relevant residential purpose (the sole or main residence of at least 95% of its residents). A non-qualifying building is a building which is not designed as a qualifying building i.e. a commercial, non-residential building. All supplies of construction services which are not subject to the reduced-rate or zero-rated are standard-rated including all works on non-qualifying buildings (i.e. commercial buildings such as offices, factories or warehouses) or where any work requires a certificate of intended use for VAT purposes a subcontractor must standard-rate their services (including buildings to be used for a relevant charitable purpose or a relevant residential purpose and conversion services supplied to relevant housing associations). Subcontractors' services, goods and building materials and related professional services are also standard-rated in relation to non-qualifying buildings.

5.9.1   Residential accommodation

Zero-rating applies to services supplied in the course of construction of a new dwelling or dwellings (and which relate to the construction). This also includes building materials and certain electrical goods incorporated into a building by a builder who is also supplying the zero-rated services, garages where these are attached to a dwelling and constructed at the same time, and civil engineering works in relation to serviced plots where these are closely connected to the construction of qualifying buildings and where the construction of the qualifying buildings will follow on closely after the completion of the works. The zero-rating also applies to articles ordinarily incorporated by builders in that type of building but not electrical and gas appliances except ventilation and air cooling systems, burglar or fire alarms, waste disposal units or compactors (in blocks of flats), lifts or hoists, but not free-standing appliances or free-standing furniture.

Specifically standard-rated in relation to new dwellings are the separate supply of architectural, surveying or consultancy or supervisory services, the hire of goods on their own e.g. plant and machinery without an operator, scaffolding without erection/dismantling.

5.9.2 Relevant residential purpose

Zero-rating also applies to construction of new buildings for a relevant residential purpose. Zero-rating does not apply until the customer has given the builder a certificate of intended use. Subcontractors' services are standard-rated because for zero-rating to apply the supply must be to the person who intends to use the building and subcontractors' services are supplied to a main contractor or other intermediary rather than the person who intends to use the building.

A relevant residential purpose includes residential accommodation for students or children, a residence which is the sole or main residence of at least 90% of its residents such as a home or other institution providing residential accommodation for children or personal care for persons in need, a hospice, a monastery, nunnery or similar establishment but excluding use as a hospital, prison or similar institution, and excluding use as a hotel, inn or similar establishment.

Apportionment applies to partly-residential buildings and generally supplies of services to the qualifying part are zero-rated, supplies of services to the non-qualifying part are standard-rated. In general the zero rating only applies to the part which is a dwelling or is residential (except communal areas in residential flats).

5.9.3 Relevant charitable purpose

Zero-rating also applies to construction of new buildings for a relevant charitable purpose, a building which is used by a charity for at least 95% for non-business purposes. Zero-rating does not apply until the customer has given the builder a certificate of intended use. Subcontractors' services are standard-rated because for zero-rating the supply must be to the person who intends to use the building and subcontractors' services are supplied to a main contractor or other intermediary rather than the person who intends to use the building. A relevant charitable purpose includes use by as a charity otherwise than in the course or furtherance of a business such as places of worship, school buildings where no fee is charged, grant-funded research buildings, village or community halls, scout or guide huts, annexes which are capable of functioning independently from the main building and where the main access is not via the existing building. Apportionment applies to partly charitable buildings and generally supplies of services to the qualifying part are zero-rated, supplies of services to the non-qualifying part are standard-rated.

5.9.4 Protected buildings

A protected building is a listed building or a scheduled monument and which is or will be a qualifying building after reconstruction. Until 1 October 2012 the supply of services in the course of an approved alteration was zero-rated but from 1 October 2012 the supply of services in the course of alteration or reconstruction is standard-rated. Zero-rating continues to apply until 30 September 2015 under transitional rules which apply to the first grant of a major interest in a substantially reconstructed protected building where 60% of the work (by cost) relates to approved alterations: if those approved alterations are within the scope of a relevant consent applied for before 21 March 2012; or of a written contract entered into before 21 March 2012; or if 10% of the substantial reconstruction (measured by cost) was completed prior to 21 March 2012.

5.9.5 Civil engineering works

Construction services related to civil engineering works (e.g. roads, bridges and tunnels) are standard-rated including subcontractors' services, goods and building materials and related professional services except where these relate to qualifying buildings (e.g. utilities or road works as part of a residential development) or residential caravan parks (zero-rated).

5.9.6 Residential conversions

Services supplied to housing associations (registered social landlords) in the course of conversion are zero-rated in relation to a non-residential building or part thereof converted into a residential building designed as a dwelling or dwellings or intended for use for a relevant residential purpose. The zero-rating includes including building materials and certain electrical goods but not related professional services or the hire of goods or the services of subcontractors.

Qualifying services supplied in the course of a qualifying conversion are reduced-rate. A qualifying conversion is the conversion of a single household to multiple occupancy or relevant residential purpose, multiple occupancy into single household or relevant residential purpose, relevant residential purpose into single household or multiple occupancy or any other building to single household, multiple occupancy or relevant residential purpose.

Qualifying services include carrying out work to the fabric of the building, carrying out work within the immediate site of the building related to utilities, drainage or waste disposal etc, including all repair and maintenance, decoration or improvement. Subcontractors' services are reduced-rate except in relation to a relevant residential purpose (standard-rated). The reduced-rate applies to articles ordinarily incorporated by builders in that type of building but not electrical and gas appliances except ventilation and air cooling systems, burglar or fire alarms, waste disposal units or compactors (in blocks of flats), lifts or hoists.

Specifically standard-rated in relation to qualifying conversions are the separate supply of architectural, surveying or consultancy or supervisory services, the hire of goods on their own e.g. plant and machinery without an operator, scaffolding without erection/dismantling.

5.9.7   Other reduced-rate supplies

The reduced-rate applies to the renovation or alteration of a single household dwelling that has not been lived in for two years or more, a multiple occupancy dwelling that has not been lived in for two years or more, or a building to be used for a relevant residential purpose that has not been lived in for two years or more. Where the property has not been empty for two years or more any renovations or alterations would be standard-rated. The reduced-rate also applies to supplies of services by installers of energy saving materials including supplies of energy saving materials such as insulation, draught stripping and solar panels and also heat pumps, wind turbines and water turbines. And to supplies to a qualifying person of heating appliances and installation services funded by a grant under a relevant scheme. A qualifying person is a person in receipt of benefits and a relevant scheme is one sponsored by a public body. And to the supply of services of installing mobility aids and the supply of mobility aids by a person installing them for use in domestic accommodation by a person aged 60 years or over.

(see *VAT Notice 708 Buildings & Construction*)

LAND AND PROPERTY

6   International VAT

6.1   Place of Taxation

The VAT liability of international transactions depends on whether the supply is one of goods or services and whether it is within the EU (the term EC is still in use in relation to VAT e.g. EC Sales List or intra-EC transactions) or outside (and if within the EU whether the place of taxation is the UK). The concept of import and export now only applies to non-EU transactions i.e. imports from outside the EU and exports outside the EU. Within the EU Single Market movements of goods are described as acquisitions (or arrivals) by the purchasing business and removals (or dispatches) by the selling business. There are significant differences in the rules depending on whether the supply is one of goods or services and there are general rules and special rules to determine where the supply is taxed and thus how VAT is accounted for. As a general principle, VAT is only due in one Member State where the place of taxation is within the EU.

6.2   The Single Market

The VAT territory of the EU is made up of 28 Member States (which can be checked on online or in *VAT Notice 725 The Single Market*). States such as Liechtenstein, Vatican City, Andorra and San Marino are not within the EU for VAT purposes. From a UK perspective the Isle of Man is within the EU VAT Territory but Gibraltar and the Channel Islands are not. GDs should be aware of which territories are included, or excluded, from a Member State because movements of goods between the UK and any of the above countries, or their included territories, are treated as intra-EC supplies for VAT purposes, whereas movements of goods between the UK and any of the excluded territories are treated as imported or exported goods for VAT purposes.

The EU VAT Territory currently consists of:

- Austria
- Belgium
- Bulgaria
- Croatia
- Cyprus
- Czech Republic
- Denmark, except the Faroe Islands and Greenland
- Estonia
- Finland
- France, including Monaco
- Germany, except Busingen and the Isle of Heligoland

- Greece
- Hungary
- The Republic of Ireland
- Italy, except the communes of Livigno and Campione d'Italia and the Italian waters of Lake Lugano
- Latvia
- Lithuania
- Luxembourg
- Malta
- Netherlands
- Poland
- Portugal, including the Azores and Madeira
- Romania
- Slovakia
- Slovenia
- Spain, including the Balearic Islands but excluding Ceuta and Melilla
- Sweden
- United Kingdom, including the Isle of Man, but excluding the Channel Isles and Gibraltar

How VAT is accounted for on intra-EC supplies depends on whether the recipient of the supply is registered for VAT in the Member State of acquisition. Also, for these purposes movements of goods between Member States within the same legal entity (often referred to as a transfers of own goods) are treated as supplies. Special rules apply in the case of natural gas and electricity, along with heat and cooling (also heat and cooling).

An EC Sales List (ESL) is required if supplies of goods or services are made to taxable persons in other Member States. If Box 8 of the VAT Return is completed HMRC will automatically send an ESL to complete. The system for collecting statistics on the trade in goods between Member States is known as Intrastat. All businesses carrying out trade with other Member States (including GDs) must declare the totals of their sales and acquisitions on their VAT Return. Businesses whose EU trade exceeds a legally set threshold have to complete additional statistical information called Supplementary Declarations. Statistics are compiled from the Supplementary Declarations and information supplied on the VAT Return.

(see *VAT Notice 725 The Single Market*)

6.3   Acquisitions & Removals

Where goods are removed from one Member State and acquired in another the general rule is that output tax is not chargeable by the removing taxable person to an acquiring taxable person. The acquiring taxable person accounts for VAT at the rate in force in the Member State of acquisition. In practice in the UK this means that the VAT on acquisitions is accounted for in Box 2 of the VAT Return and if allowable Input tax, also in Box 4. If not allowable Input tax the effect is to rebalance the acquisition in relation to partial exemption and non-business activities by excluding the VAT claim in Box 4.

For example, if a GD purchases goods or equipment from another Member State the VAT which would have been chargeable if purchased in the UK is added (in Box 2) to the output tax (Box 1) of the GD's VAT Return and forms part of the total in Box 3. If the goods or equipment relates to the non-business activities of the GD no allowable input tax entitlement would arise and no VAT would be claimed in Box 4 resulting in the same outcome as if the goods or equipment had been purchased in the UK.

(see *VAT Notice 725 The Single Market*)

6.3.1 Acquisitions
An acquisition in the UK occurs where:
- there is an intra-EC movement of goods to the UK;
- the goods are received here by a VAT registered trader; and
- the supplier is registered for VAT in the Member State of departure,
in which case the recipient is required to account for VAT on the goods acquired in the UK.

A GD must account for any tax due on the VAT Return for the period in which the tax point occurs and it may treat this as input tax on the same VAT Return subject to the normal rules.

The time of acquisition is the earlier of either:
- the 15th day of the month following the one in which the goods were sent; or
- the date the supplier issued their invoice.

Acquisitions are liable at the same rate as domestic supplies of identical goods in the UK. So, for example, no tax is due on acquisitions of goods which are currently zero-rated in the UK. Part or full payment for an intra-EC supply of goods does not create a tax point for the acquisition. The VAT on an acquisition is always due in the Member State where the goods are received. However, there is a fallback provision that applies where the VAT registration number quoted to the supplier to secure zero-rating has been issued in a different Member State. In that event the acquisition tax must be accounted for in the Member State of registration, but the customer also remains liable to account for acquisition VAT in the Member State to which the goods have been sent.

(see *VAT Notice 725 The Single Market*)

6.3.2   Removals

The normal VAT treatment of goods supplied between taxable persons in different Member States is that the removal in the Member State of dispatch is zero-rated, and VAT is due on the acquisition of the goods in the Member State of arrival and is accounted for by the recipient on their VAT Return at the rate in force in that Member State (Box 2 of the UK VAT Return). Goods sent to the Isle of Man from the UK are treated as domestic supplies for VAT purposes therefore VAT must be charged at the appropriate UK rate in the normal way. But goods sent to the Channel Islands or Gibraltar are treated as exports from the EU for VAT purposes (the EU VAT Territory includes the Isle of Man but not the Channel Islands or Gibraltar).

The tax point for a supply of goods to a taxable person in another Member State is the earlier of either the 15th day of the month following the one in which it sends the goods to a business customer (or a business customer takes them away), or the date it issues a VAT invoice for the supply. Businesses should use the tax point as the reference date for including the supplies on the VAT Return, EC Sales Lists and, normally, the Intrastat Supplementary Declarations. The receipt of a payment in these circumstances does not create a tax point for the intra-EC supply. However, a business must issue a VAT invoice to a business customer for the amount paid to it and the date of issue of the VAT invoice will be the tax point. Where a business issues a series of invoices relating to the same supply of goods, the time limit for obtaining valid evidence of removal begins from the date of the final invoice.

(see *VAT Notice 725 The Single Market*)

6.3.3   Zero-rating

Article 28C(A) of the EC Sixth Directive (77/388/EEC) allows Member States to exempt certain supplies subject to conditions laid down for the purpose of ensuring the correct application of such exemptions (zero-rating) and preventing any evasion, avoidance or abuse. The UK uses the term 'zero-rating' rather than 'exemption' used in EU law to avoid confusion with the use of exemption elsewhere in UK law. A supply from the UK to a customer in another Member State is zero-rated where a business obtains and shows on a VAT sales invoice the recipient's EC VAT registration number, including the 2-letter country prefix code, and the goods are sent or transported out of the UK to a destination in another Member State, and a business obtains and retains valid commercial evidence that the goods have been removed from the UK within the time limits.

A business cannot zero-rate a sale, even if the goods are subsequently removed to another Member State, if it supplies the goods to a UK VAT registered recipient (unless that recipient is also registered for VAT in another Member State – in such cases they must provide their EC VAT registration number and the goods must be removed to another Member State), delivers to, or allow the goods to be collected by, a UK recipient at a UK address, or allows the goods to be used in the UK in the period between supply and removal, except where specifically authorised to do so. The time limits for removing the goods and obtaining valid evidence of removal will begin from the time of supply. For goods removed to another Member State the time limits are three months (including supplies of goods involved in groupage or consolidation prior to removal), or six months for supplies of goods involved in processing or incorporation prior to removal.

HMRC advise that when a business makes a supply of goods to a taxable person in another Member State, but has to deliver them to a third party in the UK which is also making a taxable supply of goods or services to that recipient, a business can zero-rate the supply provided:
- it obtains and show on the VAT sales invoice the customer's EC VAT registration number, including the 2-letter country prefix code,
- the goods are only being delivered and not supplied to the third person in the UK,
- no use is made of the goods other than for processing or incorporation into other goods for removal, and
- it obtains and keeps valid commercial evidence that the goods have been removed from the UK within the time limits,

and the business records show:
- the name, address and VAT number of the customer in the EC,
- the invoice number and date,
- the description, quantity and value of the goods,
- the name and address of the third person in the UK to whom the goods were delivered,
- the date by which the goods must be removed,
- proof of removal obtained from the person responsible for transporting the goods out of the UK, and
- the date the goods were actually removed from the UK.

The business records must be able to show that the goods supplied have been processed or incorporated into the goods removed from the UK.

In cases where the third party is not in the UK but in another Member State, the same conditions will generally apply to allow a business to zero-rate the supply. If a business cannot obtain and show a valid EC VAT registration number on its sales invoice it must charge and account for output tax in the UK at the appropriate UK rate. If the goods are not removed or a business does not have the evidence of removal within the time limits it must account for VAT. No VAT is due on goods which would normally be zero-rated when supplied in the UK.

HMRC also advise that businesses should carry out normal commercial checks such as bank and trade credit-worthiness references before it starts making supplies to an EU customer. As part of these checks it should ask the customer to supply their EC VAT registration number. If they do not supply the EC VAT registration number then a business is obliged to charge UK VAT on any supplies of goods. If it is supplying services and its customer cannot supply an EC VAT registration number then it must make sure there is sufficient evidence to show that the supply is to a business in order to zero-rate the supply. Businesses should check the validity of the EC VAT registration number using the Europa Website. All Member States share these arrangements and businesses in other Member States can verify a UK VAT registration number in the same way.

http://europa.eu/youreurope/business/vat-customs/check-number-vies/

(see *VAT Notice 725 The Single Market*)

6.3.4   Evidence of removal
HMRC require evidence that a supply has taken place and the goods have been removed from the UK and recommend that a combination of the following documents are retained:
• the customer's order (including customer's name, VAT number and delivery address for the goods);
• inter-company correspondence;
• copy sales invoice (including a description of the goods, an invoice number and customer's EC VAT number etc);
• advice note;
• packing list;
• commercial transport document(s) from the carrier responsible for removing the goods from the UK, for example an International Consignment Note (CMR) fully completed by the consignor, the haulier and signed by receiving consignee;

- details of insurance or freight charges;
- bank statements as evidence of payment;
- receipted copy of the consignment note as evidence of receipt of goods abroad;
- any other documents relevant to the removal of the goods in question which it would normally obtain in the course of its intra-EC business.

Photocopy certificates of shipment or other transport documents are not normally acceptable as evidence of removal unless authenticated with an original stamp and dated by an authorised official of the issuing office.

The documents a business uses as proof of removal must clearly identify the following:

- the supplier;
- the consignor (where different from the supplier);
- the customer;
- the goods;
- an accurate value;
- the mode of transport and route of movement of the goods; and
- the EC destination.

If a taxable person in another Member State is arranging removal of the goods from the UK directly it can be difficult for a UK business as the supplier to obtain adequate proof of removal as the carrier is contracted to the recipient in the other Member State. Before zero-rating the supply a business must ascertain what evidence of removal of the goods from the UK will be provided. Evidence must show that the goods it supplied have left the UK. Copies of transport documents alone will not be sufficient. Information held must identify the date and route of the movement of goods and the mode of transport involved.

A business must make sure that the proof of removal is:

- retained for six years; and
- made readily available so that any VAT assurance officer is able to substantiate the zero-rating of removals.

A business, as the supplier of the goods, or the customer can appoint a freight forwarder, shipping company, airline or other person to handle its intra-EC supplies and produce the necessary evidence of removal. However, it remains legally responsible for ensuring that the conditions for zero-rating supplies of goods to other Member States are met. This includes obtaining and holding evidence of removal of the goods from the UK.

If a business uses a freight forwarder, consignments (often coming from several consignors) may be aggregated into one load, known as groupage or consolidation cargo. The freight forwarder must keep copies of the original bill of lading, sea-waybill or air-waybill, and all consignments in the load must be shown on the container or vehicle manifest. A business will be issued with a certificate of shipment by the freight forwarder, often supported by an authenticated photocopy of the original bill of lading, a sea-waybill or a house air-waybill. Where such consignments are being removed, the forwarder may be shown as the consignor in the shipping documents.

(a) Certificate of shipment

Certificates of shipment are usually produced by packers and consolidators involved in road, rail and sea groupage consignments when they themselves receive only a single authenticated transport document from the carrier. It is an important document, which should be sent as soon as the goods have been removed from the UK. The certificate of shipment must be an original and authenticated by an official of the issuing company unless it is computer produced, on a once-only basis, as a by-product of the issuing company's accounting system. A properly completed certificate of shipment will help businesses to meet the evidential requirements.

(b) What information must be shown?

Although the certificate of shipment can be in any format, it must be an original and will usually contain the following information:

- the name and address of the issuing company
- a unique reference number or issuer's file reference
- the name of the supplier of the goods (and VAT number if known)
- the place, port or airport of loading
- the place, port or airport of shipment
- the name of the ship or the aircraft flight prefix and number
- the date of sailing or flight
- the customer's name
- the destination of the goods
- a full description of the goods removed to another Member State (including quantity, weight and value)
- the number of packages
- the supplier's invoice number and date if known
- the bill of lading or air-waybill number (if applicable)
- the identifying number of the vehicle, container or railway wagon

Goods sent by post may be zero-rated if they are sent directly to a taxable person in another Member State, and the business holds the necessary evidence of posting.

(see *VAT Notice 725 The Single Market*)

6.4   Imports & Exports

6.4.1   Imports

VAT is charged and payable on the importation of goods into the UK from outside the EU but payable directly as part of the importation process and not as output tax in the VAT Return. It can, however, if allowable, be recovered as input tax in Box 4 of the VAT Return. Again, if not allowable input tax the effect is to rebalance the position in relation to partial exemption and non-business activities by excluding the input tax claim in Box 4.

There are various reliefs on the import VAT charge including on:

*   zero-rated goods under Schedule 8 VAT Act 1994 (see **Appendix 8 – Zero-Rated Supplies**);
*   goods to be used for examination, analysis or test purposes;
*   biological or chemical substances or animals for laboratory use in a relevant establishment;
*   human blood and tissue products; and
*   medical equipment funded by charities.

(see *VAT Notice 702 Imports*)

6.4.2   Exports

Goods which are supplied outside the EU are held to be consumed outside the EU and, therefore, not taxed within the EU and are zero-rated. An exporter is a person who, for VAT purposes either supplies or owns goods and exports or arranges for them to be exported to a destination outside the EU, or supplies goods to an overseas person, who arranges for the goods to be exported to a destination outside the EU. A direct export occurs when the supplier send goods to a destination outside the EU and it is responsible either for arranging the transport itself or appointing a freight agent. An indirect export occurs when an overseas customer or their agent collects or arranges for the collection of the goods from a supplier within the UK and then takes them outside the EU.

A business must meet certain conditions before it can zero-rate supplies of goods for export including in relation to evidence (either official or commercial) it must hold to prove entitlement to zero-rating, the time limits in which the goods must be exported from the EU and the time limits in which it must obtain evidence of export to support zero-rating and only exports that comply with these conditions are eligible for zero-rating. The time limit for direct and indirect exports of goods (and obtaining evidence of export) is three months i.e. the goods must be exported within three months of the supply or VAT must be charged and for goods involved in processing or incorporation prior to export (and obtaining evidence of export) the time limit is six months or VAT must be charged.

The evidence to be retained as proof of export (whether official or commercial or supporting) must clearly identify:
- the supplier
- the consignor (where different from the supplier)
- the customer
- the goods
- an accurate value
- the export destination, and
- the mode of transport and route of the export movement

HMRC accept that if the overseas customer arranges the export of the goods from the UK it can be difficult for a UK business as the supplier to obtain adequate proof of export as the carrier is contracted to the overseas customer. Before zero-rating the supply a business must ascertain what evidence of export of the goods from the UK will be provided. The evidence must show that the goods supplied have left the UK. HMRC advise that if the evidence of export does not show that the goods have left the EU within the appropriate time limits, or is found upon examination to be unsatisfactory, the supplier will become liable for payment of the VAT.

Evidence of export may include the following:
- a written order from your customer which shows their name and address, and the address where the goods are to be delivered;
- copy sales invoice showing the invoice number, customer's name and a description of the goods;
- delivery address for the goods;
- date of departure of goods from your premises and from the EC;
- name and address of the haulier collecting the goods; registration number of the vehicle collecting the goods and the name and signature of the driver;
- where the goods are to be taken out of the EC by an alternative haulier or vehicle, the name and address of that haulier, the registration number of the vehicle and a signature for the goods;
- route, for example, Channel Tunnel, port of exit;
- copy of travel tickets; and
- name of ferry or shipping company and date of sailing or airway number and airport.

Export documentation must be kept for six years and made readily available to any visiting VAT Officer. If the correct export evidence is not obtained within the appropriate time limits then the goods supplied become subject to VAT.

6.4.3 Foreign & Commonwealth Office (FCO), Ministry of Defence (MOD) and Overseas Authorities

The supply of goods ordered by British Embassies, High Commissions and diplomats abroad that are delivered to the Foreign & Commonwealth Office (FCO) for export through diplomatic channels (within three months) of the time of supply can be zero-rated. To evidence that the supply was made to an overseas person a business must be able to identify the destination of the goods. Documents which contain this information should be retained and a certificate of receipt from the FCO must be obtained within three months of the time of the supply of goods. Supplies to the FCO in the UK are subject to the normal rules. Supplies of goods to GDs other than the FCO can be zero-rated if there is a direct export to a destination outside the EU and subject to the normal rules. Supplies to GDs in the UK are subject to the normal rules even if the goods are ordered for, or by, overseas establishments.

The normal rules also apply to supplies of goods or services to the Ministry of Defence (MOD) in the UK. However, direct exports to overseas military and similar installations may be zero-rated provided with the relevant conditions for export are complied with.

Special conditions exist to allow the zero-rating of supplies of goods where a military unit is about to be posted to a location outside the EU.

The supply of goods (except new and second-hand motor vehicles) to regimental shops can be zero-rated provided:

- each written order received from the President of the Regimental Institute (PRI) states that the regiment is about to take up an overseas posting and that the goods ordered will be exported from the EU;
- the goods are delivered to the PRI ready packed for shipment no more than 48 hours before the regiment is due to depart for the overseas posting;
- the goods are exported outside the EU; and
- a certificate of receipt signed by the PRI is retained which clearly identifies the goods, gives full shipment details and states the date on which they were exported from the EU.

The PRI will keep a full record of such transactions for reference purposes for a period of not less than six years.

Supplies of goods to overseas authorities which are ordered through their embassies, High Commissions or purchasing agents in the UK can be zero-rated provided:

- a separate record of each transaction is kept, including evidence that the supply has been made to an overseas authority, for example the order for the goods, sales invoice made out to the overseas authority, evidence of payment from the overseas authority etc;
- the goods are exported and proof of export obtained within three months; and
- the goods are not used between the time of leaving the supplier's premises and export, either for their normal purpose or for display, exhibition or copying.

(see *VAT Notice 703 Exports*)

6.5 Place of Supply of Services

For VAT purposes, the place of supply of services is the place where a service is treated as being supplied. This is the place where it is liable to VAT (if any). There are general and special rules to determine where services are supplied. Where the place of supply of services is in a Member State that supply is subject to the VAT rules of that Member State and not those of any other country. If the Member State is not the UK the supply is outside the scope of UK VAT. Where the place of supply of services is outside the EU, that supply is made outside the EU and is therefore not liable to VAT in any Member State (although local taxes may apply). Such a supply is outside the scope of both UK and EU VAT. If the place of supply of services is the UK, a business must charge UK VAT and account for it regardless of where the customer belongs. If the place of supply of is another Member State, the business or the customer may be liable to account for any VAT due to the tax authorities of that Member State (reverse charge).

6.5.1 Place of belonging

UK law refers to 'belonging' whereas EU law refers to 'establishment' but these two terms have the same meaning for VAT purposes. For certain types of supply the place where a supplier or customer belongs determines where services are supplied and which of them accounts for any VAT due. The place of supply of land-related services is where the land is located. The place of supply of 'where performed' services is generally the place of performance. Therefore, the place of belonging of either the supplier or the customer does not affect the place of supply of these services.

A business belongs in the UK for the purposes of either making or receiving supplies of services when any of the following apply:

- it has a business establishment or some other fixed establishment in the UK and none elsewhere;
- it has a business establishment in the UK and fixed establishments in other countries, but the UK establishment is most directly connected with making or receiving the supplies in question;
- it has a fixed establishment in the UK and a business establishment and/or fixed establishments overseas, but the UK establishment is most directly connected with making or receiving the supplies in question; or
- it has no business or fixed establishment anywhere, but the usual place of residence is the UK.

The business establishment is the principal place of business and is usually the head office, headquarters or 'seat' from which the business is run. There can be only one such place which may be an office, showroom or factory.

(see *VAT Notice 741A Place of Supply of Services*)

6.5.2   General rules

From 1 January 2010 there are two general rules for the place of supply of services, one for business to business (B2B) and one for business to consumer (B2C) supplies. There are also special place of supply rules for certain services. The B2B general rule for supplies of services is that the supply is made where the customer belongs. The B2C general rule for supplies of services is that the supply is made where the supplier belongs. For place of supply of services purposes 'B2B supplies' means supplies to businesses whose activities are wholly of a business nature. It also includes supplies to entities which have both business and non-business activities such as charities and GDs. For place of supply of services purposes 'B2C supplies' means supplies to a private individual, a charity, a public or other body which has no business activities or a 'person' who receives a supply of services wholly for private purposes.

(see *VAT Notice 741A Place of Supply of Services*)

6.5.3   The reverse charge

The reverse charge on the supply of services arises where the place of supply of services from a non-UK supplier is deemed to be the UK and the effect is to put the UK taxable person in the same position as if they had received the supply from a UK supplier. If the place of supply is the UK, the output tax due on the supply is accounted for in the UK recipient taxable person's VAT Return in Box 1 and if allowable input tax, also in Box 4. If not allowable input, tax the effect is to rebalance the position in relation to partial exemption and non-business activities by excluding the input tax claim in Box 4. The reverse charge does not apply to zero-rated or exempt supplies received (the place of supply is the UK and therefore the liability is that of the UK).

The key to the reverse charge is the place of supply. The general rule following significant changes effective from 1 January 2010 is that the place of supply for business to business supplies (which includes GDs) is the place where the recipient taxable person is established (previously it was where the supplier was established). The place of supply is the only place the supply can be taxed. If outside the UK but within the EU, the supply is outside the scope of UK VAT but will be taxed in the other Member State, and if outside the EU it cannot be liable to VAT in any Member State. For example, if a GD provided general rule services to a business based in another Member State then the output tax would be due in the other Member State not in the UK. The supply would be outside the scope of UK VAT but any VAT incurred by the GD in making the supply would be allowable Input tax under VAT Act 1994 s.26. Conversely, if a GD was the recipient of the supply the output tax would be due in the UK and accounted for in Box 1 of the GD's VAT Return and if allowable input tax, also in Box 4 (the net value of a reverse charge supply is accounted for in Boxes 6 and 7).

(see *VAT Notice 741A Place of Supply of Services*)

6.5.4 Services relating to land
Services related to land are not subject to the general rules on the place of supply of services. The place of supply of services related to land is where the land itself is located irrespective of where it or the customer belongs.

Land includes all forms of land and property; growing crops, buildings, walls, fences, civil engineering works or other structures fixed permanently to the land or seabed. It also covers plant, machinery or equipment which is an installation or edifice in its own right, for example, a refinery or fixed oil/gas production platform. Machinery installed in buildings other than as a fixture is normally not regarded as 'land' but as 'goods'.

HMRC give the following examples of land-related services:
- the supply of hotel accommodation;
- the provision of a site for a stand at an exhibition where the exhibitor obtains the right to a defined area of the exhibition hall;

- services supplied in the course of construction, conversion, enlargement, reconstruction, alteration, demolition, repair or maintenance (including painting and decorating) of any building or civil engineering work;
- the supply of plant or machinery, together with an operator, for work on a construction site;
- services of estate agents, auctioneers, architects, solicitors, surveyors, engineers and similar professional people relating to land, buildings or civil engineering works. This includes the management, conveyancing, survey or valuation of property by a solicitor, surveyor or loss adjuster;
- services connected with oil/gas/mineral exploration or exploitation relating to specific sites of land or the seabed;
- the surveying (such as seismic, geological or geomagnetic) of land or seabed, including associated data processing services to collate the required information;
- legal services such as conveyancing or dealing with applications for planning permission;
- packages of property management services which may include rent collection, arranging repairs and the maintenance of financial accounts; and
- the supply of warehouse space.

This place of supply rule applies only to services which relate directly to specific sites or specified land or property. It does not apply if a supply of services has only an indirect connection with land, or if the land-related service is only an incidental component of a more comprehensive supply of services.

HMRC give the following examples of services which are not land-related:
- repair and maintenance of machinery which is not installed as a fixture;
- the hiring out of civil engineering plant on its own, which is the letting on hire of goods;
- the secondment of staff to a building site, which is a supply of staff;
- the legal administration of a deceased person's estate which happens to include property. These are lawyers' services;
- advice or information relating to land prices or property markets because they do not relate to specific sites;
- feasibility studies assessing the potential of particular businesses or business potential in a geographic area. Such services do not relate to a specific property or site;
- provision of a recording studio where technicians are included as part of the supply. These are engineering services; and

- services of an accountant in simply calculating a tax return from figures provided by a client, even where those figures relate to rental income.

If a taxable person registered in the UK is a recipient of these services in relation to land situated in the UK it may be required to account for the reverse charge if the supplier belongs outside the UK. If a business is a supplier who does not belong in the UK, and the customer is not registered for UK VAT, the business, as the supplier, is responsible for accounting for any UK VAT due on the supply. If a business is not already registered in the UK, it may be liable to register as a non-established taxable person. Equally, if a taxable person registered in the UK supplies services relating to land in another Member State it may be liable to register for VAT in that Member State.

6.5.5 Services supplied where performed
The place of supply of events or performance is where the event or performance takes place:

- services of sportspersons appearing in exhibition matches, races or other forms of competition;
- provision of race prepared cars including the hire of the car and support services to ensure optimum maintenance and operation of the car throughout a series of races;
- scientific services of technicians carrying out tests or experiments in order to obtain data;
- services of an actor or singer, whether or not in front of a live audience;
- services relating to conferences or meetings;
- services of an oral interpreter at an event, such as a meeting;
- the right to participate in an exhibition or the provision of an undefined site for a stand at an exhibition;
- services relating to a specific exhibition including carpenters and electricians erecting and fitting out stands at exhibition venues; and
- educational and training services although such services may be exempt when supplied in the UK.

(see *VAT Notice 741A Place of Supply of Services*)

6.6 Overseas Governments
As an extra-statutory concession training services supplied in the UK to overseas governments for the purposes of their sovereign activities are zero-rated. The relief does not apply if services are received for business purposes. It therefore excludes the training of personnel from government-owned industries or sponsored commercial organisations such as state

airlines or nationalised industries. However, such businesses may otherwise be able to claim a refund of VAT incurred in the UK in relation to business activities under the normal rules.

If a business supplies taxable training services to foreign or overseas governments the supply is zero-rated provided the services are used by the foreign or overseas government for the furtherance of its sovereign activities (i.e. not for business purposes), and a written statement from the foreign or overseas government concerned, or its accredited representative, certifying that the trainees are employed in furtherance of its sovereign activities is obtained and retained. A foreign or overseas government includes overseas government officials, public servants and members of organisations such as the armed forces, the police, the emergency services and similar bodies answerable to the government concerned. Zero-rating only applies to the supply of the actual training and does not extend to any associated services which are supplied separately, such as accommodation or transport nor does it apply to training services which would otherwise be exempt (e.g. education or training provided by an eligible body under *VAT Act 1994 Schedule 9 Group 6 – Education*).

6.7   VAT MOSS 2015

From 1 January 2015 the rules on the place of supply of business to consumer digital services (broadcasting, telecommunications and e-services) changed. The place of taxation is now determined by the location of the consumer. Previously, where digital services were supplied on a B2C basis the supplier was responsible for accounting for VAT on the supply. The new rules only apply where a UK business meets all of the following criteria: it supplies digital services from the UK to another Member State (goods and non-digital services sold over the internet are not within scope); it supplies those services to a private consumer in another Member State; and, charges for that supply (digital services provided free of charge are outside the scope of VAT). Businesses outside the EU (for example, the USA) supplying digital services to consumers in one or more Member State are also affected by the changes. The new place of supply rule for B2C supplies of digital services is a special rule and supersedes the general B2C place of supply rule. A business must determine whether the service is a digital service, the status of the customer i.e. business or non-business, the place of supply (i.e. the Member State) and whether the supply must be taxed at the Member State's standard or reduced VAT rate, or whether it is eligible for any VAT exemptions (e.g. most Member States exempt betting and gaming).

6.7.1 Digital services

Digital services include broadcasting, telecommunications and electronically supplied services. Broadcasting services include the supply of audio and audio-visual content for simultaneous listening or viewing by the general public on the basis of a programme schedule by a person that has editorial responsibility and live streaming via the internet if broadcast at the same time as transmission via radio or television.

Telecommunications services means transmission of signals of any nature by wire, optical, electromagnetic or other system and includes fixed and mobile telephone services for the transmission and switching of voice, data and video, including telephone services with an imaging component, otherwise known as videophone services, telephone services provided through the Internet, including Voice over Internet Protocol (VoIP), voice mail, call waiting, call forwarding, caller identification, three-way calling and other call management services, paging services or access to the internet but does not include services provided over the telephone, such as call centre helpdesk services.

The rule change only applies to 'e-services' that are 'electronically supplied' and includes things like:
- supplies of images or text, such as photos, screensavers, e-books and other digitised documents e.g. PDF files;
- supplies of music, films and games, including games of chance and gambling games, and of programmes on demand;
- online magazines;
- website supply or web hosting services;
- distance maintenance of programmes and equipment;
- supplies of software and software updates; and
- advertising space on a website.

Sales not affected by the change include:
- using the internet, or some electronic means of communication, merely to communicate or facilitate trading;
- supplies of goods, where the order and processing is done electronically;
- supplies of physical books, newsletters, newspapers or journals;
- services of lawyers and financial consultants who advise clients through email;
- booking services or tickets to entertainment events, hotel accommodation or car hire;

- educational or professional courses, where the content is delivered by a teacher over the internet or an electronic network (in other words, using a remote link);
- offline physical repair services of computer equipment; and
- advertising services in newspapers, on posters and on television.

Apart from those businesses who sell digital services entirely through digital platforms, or marketplaces who take on responsibility for accounting for the VAT due, businesses must consider how they intend to account for the VAT on these supplies.

Businesses will have to make one of the following choices and either:

- register to use the UK VAT Mini One Stop Shop (VAT MOSS) allowing the business to account for VAT due in other Member States in the UK via HMRC; or
- register for VAT in every Member State where it makes digital supplies to consumers, and file returns and make payments to the tax authorities in each of those Member States.

HMRC recommends that businesses making these types of supply register for and use UK VAT MOSS. The alternative is to register in each Member State where supplies are made irrespective of value.

Appendix 1: VAT Act 1994, section 41

Part III - Application of Act in particular cases

41 Application to the Crown

(1) This Act shall apply in relation to taxable supplies by the Crown as it applies in relation to taxable supplies by taxable persons.

[(2) Where the supply by a Government department of any goods or services does not amount to the carrying on of a business but it appears to the Treasury that similar goods or services are or might be supplied by taxable persons in the course or furtherance of any business, then, if and to the extent that the Treasury so direct, the supply of those goods or services by that department shall be treated for the purposes of this Act as a supply in the course or furtherance of any business carried on by it.] (Repealed in Finance Act 2012)

(3) Where VAT is chargeable on the supply of goods or services to a Government department, on the acquisition of any goods by a Government department from another Member State or on the importation of any goods by a Government department from a place outside the Member States and the supply, acquisition or importation is not for the purpose —
   (a) of any business carried on by the department, or
   (b) of a supply by the department which, by virtue of section 41A, is treated as a supply in the course or furtherance of a business, then, if and to the extent that the Treasury so direct and subject to subsection (4) below, the Commissioners shall, on a claim made by the department at such time and in such form and manner as the Commissioners may determine, refund to it the amount of the VAT so chargeable.

(4) The Commissioners may make the refunding of any amount due under subsection (3) above conditional upon compliance by the claimant with requirements with respect to the keeping, preservation and production of records relating to the supply, acquisition or importation in question.

(5) For the purposes of this section goods or services obtained by one Government department from another Government department shall be treated, if and to the extent that the Treasury so direct, as supplied by that other department and similarly as regards goods or services obtained by or from the Crown Estate Commissioners.

(6) In this section "Government department" includes a Northern Ireland department, a Northern Ireland health and social services body, any body of persons exercising functions on behalf of a Minister of the Crown, including a health service body as defined in section 60(7) of the [1990 c. 19.] National Health Service and Community Care Act 1990, and any part of a Government department (as defined in the foregoing) designated for the purposes of this subsection by a direction of the Treasury.

(7) For the purposes of subsection (6) above, a National Health Service trust established under Part I of the [1990 c. 19.] National Health Service and Community Care Act 1990 or the [1978 c. 29.] National Health Service (Scotland) Act 1978 shall be regarded as a body of persons exercising functions on behalf of a Minister of the Crown.

(8) In subsection (6) "a Northern Ireland health and social services body" means—

(a) a health and social services body as defined in Article 7(6) of the [S.I.1991/194.] Health and Personal Social Services (Northern Ireland) Order 1991; and

(b) a Health and Social Services trust established under that Order.

41A Supply of goods or services by public bodies

(1) This section applies where goods or services are supplied by a body mentioned in Article 13(1) of the VAT Directive (status of public bodies as taxable persons) in the course of activities or transactions in which it is engaged as a public authority.

(2) If the supply is in respect of an activity listed in Annex I to the VAT Directive (activities in respect of which public bodies are to be taxable persons), it is to be treated for the purposes of this Act as a supply in the course or furtherance of a business unless it is on such a small scale as to be negligible.

(3) If the supply is not in respect of such an activity, it is to be treated for the purposes of this Act as a supply in the course or furtherance of a business if (and only if) not charging VAT on the supply would lead to a significant distortion of competition.

(4) In this section "the VAT Directive" means Council Directive 2006/112/EC on the common system of value added tax.

(s.41A inserted in Finance Act 2012)

Appendix 2: Treasury (Contracting-Out) Directions

Friday 10 January 2003 Treasury Value Added Tax

The Treasury direction dated 2nd December 2002 under section 41(3) of the Value Added Tax Act 1994 as to the refund to Government departments of tax charged on the supply of goods or services or on the acquisition or importation of goods by them otherwise than for the purpose of any business carried on by them or on a supply in the course or furtherance of a business.

The Treasury, in exercise of the powers conferred on them by section 41(3) of the Value Added Tax Act 1994, hereby direct as follows:

1. This direction shall come into operation on 2nd December 2002.
2. Subject as provided in paragraph 3, a Government department listed as belonging to a category of departments listed in List 1 of this direction may claim and be paid a refund of the tax charged on:
   (a) the supply to it of any services of a description in List 2;
   (b) the supply to it of leased accommodation for more than 21 years as part of the supply to it of any services of a description in List 2; or
   (c) the supply to it or acquisition from another Member State of importation from outside the Member States by it of goods closely related to the supply to it of any services of a description in List 2.
3. A tax refund as described in paragraph 2 will only be paid if:
   (a) either the supply of those services or goods is not for the purpose of:
      (i) any business carried on by the department; or
      (ii)any supply by the department which, by virtue of directions made under section 41(2) and (5) of the Value Added Tax Act 1994, is treated as a supply in the course or furtherance of a business; and
   (b)the department complies with the requirements of the Commissioners of Customs and Excise both as to the time, form and manner of making the claim and also on the keeping, preservation and production of records relating to the supply, acquisition or importation in question.
4. The Treasury direction dated 7th August 2000 is hereby revoked. Philip Woolas & Jim Fitzpatrick, Two of the Lords Commissioners of Her Majesty's Treasury. (1401/49)

Appendix 3: Treasury (Taxing) Directions

Treasury (Taxing) Directions under Section 41(2),(5) and (6) of the Value Added Tax Act 1994
Business activities of Government Departments

Treasury Directions dated 29 October 2008 under section 41(2), (5) and (6) of the Value Added Tax Act 1994 (c.23) as to the supply of goods or services by Government departments.

The Treasury, in exercise of the powers conferred on them by section 41(2), (5) and (6) of the Value Added Tax Act 1994, hereby direct as follows:

1. These Directions shall come into force on 29 October 2008.

2. In these Directions—

    "the Act" means the Value Added Tax Act 1994; "Government department" has the same meaning as in section 41(6) of the Act and includes part of a Government department designated for the purposes of that section by paragraph (3) below.

    "List 1" and "List 2" mean Lists 1 and 2 respectively in these Directions.

3. Where an entry in List 1 mentions a part of a Government department, that part is hereby designated for the purposes of section 41(6) of the Act.

4. A supply by a Government department which is mentioned in List 1 of any goods or services of a description in List 2 shall be treated for the purposes of the Act as a supply in the course or furtherance of a business carried on by that department.

5. The Treasury Directions made under section 41 (2), (5) and (6) of the Value Added Tax Act 1994 on 23 May 2002 are revoked.

D Watts

T Cunningham

Two of the Lords Commissioners of Her Majesty's Treasury

(s.41(2) repealed in Finance Act 2012 – s.41A inserted)

Appendix 4: Treasury (Contracting-Out) Directions - List of Eligible Services
(December 2002)

1. Accounting, invoicing and related services
2. Administration of the following:
   Career development loans
   Certificates of Experience
   Government support payments to the Railway Industry Pension Funds
   Grants and awards
   Services supplied under the Companies Acts and the Patent and Trademarks Acts
   Teachers' Superannuation Scheme
   Vehicle Excise Duty refunds
   Winter fuel payment scheme
   Inherited State Earnings Related Pension Scheme
   Student Loan Scheme
   Fast Track Teaching Programme
3. Administration and collection of toll charges
4. Aerial photographic surveys and aerial surveillance
5. Agricultural services of the kind normally carried out by the Farming and Rural Conservation Agency
6. Alteration, repair and maintenance of road schemes, except
   (a) any works carried out pursuant to an agreement made under section 278 of the Highways Act 1980, or (b) works involving construction on land not already used for road schemes.
7. Broadcast monitoring services
8. Cartographic services
9. Cash in transit services
10. Catering
11. Ceremonial services
12. Childcare services
13. Collection, delivery and distribution services
14. Computer Services supplied to the specification of the recipient, including the provision of a fully managed and serviced computer infrastructure
15. Conference and exhibition services
16. Debt collection
17. Departmental staff records and payroll systems including administration and payment of pensions
18. Employment advisory services as directed by the Race Relations Act 1976

19. Engineering and related process services
20. Environmental protection services of the kind normally carried out for the Department of the Environment, Food and Rural Affairs
21. Estate management services
22. Export intelligence services
23. Filming, audio-visual and production services
24. Health promotion activities
25. Hire of reprographic equipment including repair and maintenance
26. Hire of vehicles including repair and maintenance
27. Insolvency services
28. Interpretation and translation services
29. Issue of documents to, and control of, bingo halls and off-course bookmakers
30. Issue of documents under Wireless and Telegraphy Act
31. Laboratory services
32. Laundry services
33. Library services
34. Maintenance and care of livestock and fauna in connection with the Royal Parks
35. Maintenance, non-structural repair and cleaning of buildings
36. Maintenance and repair of civil engineering works
37. Maintenance, repair and cleaning of equipment, plant, vehicles and vessels
38. Maintenance and repair of statues, monuments and works of art
39. Medical and social surveys
40. Messenger, portering and reception services
41. Nursing services
42. Office removals
43. Operation and maintenance of static test facilities, engineering and support services and test range industrial support and security/safety services including those acquired for the purposes of research and development
44. Operation and maintenance of stores depots
45. Operation of hospitals, health care establishments and health care facilities and the provision of any related services
46. Operation of prisons, detention centres and remand centres, including medical services
47. Passenger transport services
48. Pest control services
49. Photographic, reprographic, graphics and design services
50. Preparation and despatch of forms
51. Press cutting services

52. Professional services, including those of any manager, adviser, expert, specialist or consultant
53. Provision under a PFI agreement of accommodation for office or other governmental use, together with management or other services in connection with that accommodation
54. Publicity services
55. Purchasing and procurement services
56. Radio services
57. Recruitment and relocation of staff and other related services
58. Research, testing, inspection, certification and approval work for the Health and Safety Executive
59. Scientific work of the kind normally carried out for the Department of the Environment, Food and Rural Affairs and the Food Standards Agency
60. Security Services
61. Services of printing, copying, reproducing or mailing any documents or publications, including typesetting services
62. Share Registry Survey
63. Storage, distribution and goods disposal services
64. Surveying, certification and registration in connection with ships and relevant record-keeping and verification, issue of certification, cards, discharge books and campaign medals to seamen
65. Training, tuition or education
66. Transport research of the kind normally carried out for the Department for Transport
67. Travel services, excluding hotel accommodation and fares
68. Travel and transport surveys, including traffic census counts
69. Typing, secretarial, telephonist and clerical services including agency staff
70. Waste disposal services
71. Welfare services
72. Careers guidance, mentoring and counselling to help people into work as part of the New Deal and ONE service
73. Services relating to Action Teams for Jobs and Employment Zones
74. Original research undertaken in order to gain knowledge and understanding
75. Inspection of woodland sites for approval of felling licence applications and of timber imports/imports using timber packing to prevent entry of foreign tree pests and diseases.

Appendix 5: Treasury (Taxing) Directions - List of Business Activities
(October 2008)

Business activities - goods and services

Accommodation, including property acquisition and disposal and any related services

Administration services

Admission to premises and to events, e.g. entertainments, air displays etc.

Advertising or publicity services

Archives

Attendance of staff at court or any similar place

Bankruptcies and insolvency services

Broadcasting services

Catering, including supplies from vending machines

Car leasing

Community tradeable emissions allowances in return for payment pursuant to section 16 of the Finance Act 2007 where such allowances could also be obtained from the private sector

Computer services or goods

Concessions for catering or other services

Conferences, exhibitions and any related facilities or services

Construction, alteration, demolition, repair or maintenance work, civil engineering work, any related services or goods

Contract or procurement services

Copying or supply of any reproductions or of any documents

Copyright, patents or licences to manufacture

Delivery or distribution services

Drainage work

Electronic transfer of data

Export of goods and related services

Filming, replay or recording services

Financial and any related services

Fishing licences or permits

Fire service assistance

Freight transport

Fuel and power

Government car service

Grant, assignment or surrender of any interest in or right over land, or of any licence to do anything in relation to land.

Grant of a right to inspect records

Goods, including goods manufactured within a Government department and sold to its staff and to other customers, stores, surplus or other equipment

Grave maintenance

Grounds maintenance

Hairdressing

Heating

Hire of vehicles, machinery or equipment, with or without operator or crew

Hydrographic, cartographic and similar services

Information or statistical services

Inspection services

Laboratory services including analysis and testing of any substance

Laundry services

Licensing, certification, authorisation or the granting of any rights other than rights over land

Manufacturing, assembling and other services

Medical services

Membership subscriptions

Meteorological and related services

Mineral or prospecting rights

Mortuary services

Nursery and day-care facilities

Occupational health services

Passenger transport

Payroll and pension administration services

Pest or animal control

Photocopying services

Photographic services

Port, airport or harbour services and related goods

Postal, packing or distribution services

Professional services, including those of any manager, adviser, expert, specialist or consultant

Publications

Radio or communication services

Recruitment services

Research, testing, experimentation, sampling or other related laboratory services

Repair or maintenance of machinery, equipment or other goods

Searches

Secondment of staff where such services could also be obtained from the private sector

APPX 5: TREASURY (TAXING) DIRECTIONS/BUSINESS ACTIVITIES

Secretarial services

Security services and related goods

Shipping services

Slaughter, rendering and disposal of animals

Social services

Statistical services, including the collection, preparation and processing of data

Storage facilities and related services

Telecommunications

Training, tuition or education and any related services or goods

Transfer of milk quota leases

Translation services

Tree planting and afforestation

Vehicle conversions

Vehicle servicing and maintenance

Verification of particulars of births, marriages or deaths

Waste disposal

Water

Weighbridge services

Appendix 6: Treasury (Taxing) Directions - List of Eligible Departments
(October 2008)

Government Departments

Advisory, Conciliation and Arbitration Service
Department of Agriculture and Rural Development
Army Base Repair Organisation
Cabinet Office
CADW (Welsh Historic Monuments)
Central Office of Information
Charity Commission
Crown Office Scotland
Crown Prosecution Service
Department of Culture, Arts and Leisure
Department for Culture, Media and Sport
Communities Scotland
Revenue and Customs
Ministry of Defence
Defence Aviation Repair Agency
Defence Science and Technology Laboratory
Driver and Vehicle Testing Agency for Northern Ireland
Department for Education and Skills
Department of Employment and Learning
Department for Enterprise, Trade and Investment
Department of the Environment
Department for Environment, Food and Rural Affairs
ESTYN (HM Inspectorate for Education and Training in Wales)
Export Credits Guarantee Department
Office of Fair Trading
Department of Finance and Personnel
Fire Authority for Northern Ireland
Fire Service College
Office of the First Minister and Deputy First Minister
Food Standards Agency
Foreign and Commonwealth Office
Forensic Science Northern Ireland
Forensic Science Service
Forestry Commission
Office of Gas and Electricity Markets
General Register Office for Scotland

Government Actuary's Department
Government Car and Dispatch Agency
Office of Government Commerce
Government Communications Bureau
Government Communications Centre
Government Communications Headquarters
Department of Health
Health Authorities (including Primary Care Groups, Local Health Groups (Wales) and Community Health Councils), Special Health Authorities, Special Health Boards (Scotland), Area Health Boards (Scotland), National Health Service Trusts, Primary Care Trusts, The Common Services Agency (Scotland), Dental Practice Board).
Health and Safety Executive
Department of Health, Social Services and Public Safety
Historic Scotland
Home Office
Hydrographic Office
Department for International Development
Land Registry
Lord Chancellor's Department
Meteorological Office
National Investment and Loans Office
Office for National Statistics
National Archives of Scotland
National Assembly for Wales
Northern Ireland Assembly
Northern Ireland Court Service
Northern Ireland Education and Library Boards
Northern Ireland Housing Executive
Northern Ireland Office
Office of the Ombudsman
OGC buying.solutions
Ordnance Survey
Ordnance Survey of Northern Ireland
Privy Council Office
Public Record Office
Public Record Office of Northern Ireland
Office for the Regulation of Electricity and Gas
Office of the Rail Regulator
Department for Regional Development
Registers of Scotland
Royal Mint

Royal Parks
Scotland Office
Scottish Executive
Scottish Parliamentary Corporate Body
Scottish Prison Service
Office of the Secretary of State for Wales
Security Service
Security Services Group
Serious Fraud Office
Department for Social Development
Office for Standards in Education (England)
Office of Telecommunications
Department of Trade and Industry
Department for Transport, Local Government and the Regions
Queen Elizabeth II Conference Centre
Treasury
Treasury Solicitor's Department
Office of Water Services
Department for Work and Pensions

Appendix 7: Reduced-Rate Supplies

Reduced-Rate Supplies

The main types of reduced-rate supplies (5%) are as follows:

Children's Car Seats
Applies to the supply, acquisition or importation of children's car seats.

Contraceptive Products
Applies to supplies of any product designed for the purposes of human contraception.

Domestic Fuel or Power
Applies to domestic (residential) use or use by a charity otherwise than in the course or furtherance of business

Energy-Saving Materials: Installation
Applies to supplies of materials by an installer and installation services.

Heating Equipment, Security Goods and Gas Supplies: Grant-Funded Installation or Connection
Applies to supplies of equipment by an installer and installation services (where grant funded).

Renovation and Alteration of Dwellings
Applies to supplies of qualifying services in the course of the renovation or alteration of certain buildings (where empty for two years or more).

Residential Conversions
Applies to supplies of qualifying services in relation to certain residential conversions.

Smoking Cessation Products
Applies to supplies of pharmaceutical products designed to help people stop smoking tobacco.

Women's Sanitary Products
Applies to supplies of products designed solely for use in collecting discharge from the womb or menstrual flow.

(any supply of goods or services in the UK is standard-rated unless specifically excluded)

Appendix 8: Zero-Rated Supplies

Zero-Rated Supplies

The main types of zero-rated supplies (0%) are as follows:

Bank Notes
Applies to the issue of bank notes.

Books etc
Applies to books and printed matter.

Caravans and Houseboats
Applies to residential caravans and houseboats (but not the supply of holiday accommodation).

Charities
Applies to the sale or letting on hire of donated goods by charities, aids for disabled persons, advertising by charities and the supply of relevant goods for medical or veterinary use or research etc.

Clothing and Footwear
Applies to children's clothing and footwear.

Construction of Buildings etc
Applies to the construction of new dwellings or buildings for a relevant residential purpose or a relevant charitable purpose.

Drugs, Medicines, Aids for the Handicapped etc.
Applies to qualifying goods.

Exports
Applies to goods which exported from the UK or removed to another EU Member State.

Food
Applies to food and groceries (but not to confectionery, soft drinks or alcohol).

Gold
Applies to supplies of gold between central banks and the London Bullion Market.

Imports
Applies to goods which would be zero-rated if supplied in the UK.

International Services

Applies to certain international services such as training supplied to an overseas government or work on goods to be exported outside the EU.

Protected Buildings

Applies to approved alterations to listed buildings (transitional period to 30th September 2015).

Sewerage Services and Water

Applies to the services of reception, disposal or treatment of foul water or the services of emptying cesspools, septic tanks or similar.

Talking Books for the Blind and Handicapped and Wireless Sets for the Blind

Applies to apparatus supplied to charities for use by blind or disabled persons.

Transport

Applies to passenger transport e.g. by bus, rail, boat or plane (but not taxis).

(any supply of goods or services in the UK is standard-rated unless specifically excluded)

Appendix 9: Exempt Supplies

Exempt Supplies

The main types of exempt supplies are as follows:

Betting, Gaming and Lotteries
Applies to games of chance and betting.

Burial and Cremation
Applies to burial and cremation services.

Cultural Services etc
Applies to cultural services provided by public bodies or not-for-profit eligible bodies.

Education
Applies to supplies of education (e.g. by schools, colleges and Universities).

Finance
Applies to credit, bank interest, share dealing, investments, insurance and other financial services.

Fund Raising Events by Charities and other Qualifying Bodies
Applies to supplies of goods and services by a charity or endowment fund in connection with a one-off fundraising event or a number of one-off events organised for charitable purposes by a charity or endowment fund.

Health and Welfare
Applies to the provision of welfare services, i.e. services directly connected with the provision of care, treatment or instruction designed to promote the physical or mental welfare of elderly, sick, distressed or disabled persons.

Insurance
(see **Finance** above).

Investment Gold
(see **Finance** above).

Land
Applies to the supply of a right over land

Postal Services
Applies to the supply of public postal services by the Royal Mail.

Sport, Sports Competitions and Physical Education

Applies to the supply of sporting services or physical recreation facilities by a not-for-profit eligible body.

Supplies of Goods where Input Tax cannot be recovered

Applies to supplies of goods where input tax is non-deductible.

Subscriptions to Trade Unions, Professional and other Public Interest Bodies

Applies to the provision of membership facilities by a professional, learned or representational association.

Works of Art etc

Applies to certain disposals of works of art including to approved bodies (such as the National Gallery).

(any supply of goods or services in the UK is standard-rated unless specifically excluded)

Appendix 10: References

Statutes
Principal VAT Directive 2006/112/EC
Value Added Tax Act 1994
VAT Regulations 1995 (SI 1995/2518)

Circulars
DAO(GEN)08/03 (HM Treasury 2003)
VAT Recovery under Headings 45 and 53 of the Contracted-Out Services Directions (HMRC 2005)
Circular HMRC 27/03/07 – Headings 14 & 37 (HMRC 2007)

Publications
VAT in the Public Sector and Exemptions in the Public Interest (EC TAXUD/2009/DE/316) (2011)
Managing Public Money (HM Treasury) (July 2013)

VAT Manuals
VATSC03100 – basic principles and underlying law: scope of vat
VATGPB2000 – bodies governed by public law
VATGPB3000 – non-business activities
VATGPB9000 – government departments and health authorities

VAT Notices
VAT Notice 700 The VAT Guide (April 2015)
VAT Notice 701/2 Welfare (July 2011)
VAT Notice 701/5 Clubs & Associations (October 2013)
VAT Notice 701/16 Water and Sewerage Services (August 2014)
VAT Notice 701/30 Education & Vocational Training (February 2014)
VAT Notice 701/40 Food Processing Services (October 2011)
VAT Notice 701/47 Culture (September 2011)
VAT Notice 701/49 Financial Services (January 2013)
VAT Notice 702 Imports (October 2014)
VAT Notice 703 Exports (March 2014)
VAT Notice 706/1 Partial Exemption (June 2011)
VAT Notice 706/2 Capital Goods Scheme (October 2011)
VAT Notice 708 Buildings & Construction (August 2014)
VAT Notice 725 The Single Market (January 2014)
VAT Notice 727 Retail Schemes (May 2012)
VAT Notice 741A Place of Supply of Services (February 2010)
VAT Notice 742 Land and Property (May 2012)
VAT Notice 742A Option to Tax (April 2014)

VAT Guidance

A Step by Step Guide to VAT Online Filing for Government Departments and NHS Trusts (HMRC 2010)

HMRC Guidance Notes for Government Departments 7th Edn 2012

Websites

www.hmrc.gov.uk

www.legislation.gov.uk

Government Departments Team

HM Revenue & Customs
Euston Tower
286 Euston Road
London
NW1 3UL

VAT Supply Team

HM Revenue & Customs
Room C3/07
100 Parliament Street
London
SW1A 2BQ

INDEX

VAT

INDEX